Glad ;
we (
wor.
~Paul E. Robinson
2022

HOPE BENEATH
THE SURFACE

Sermons For Advent,
Christmas and Epiphany
Cycle A, First Lesson Texts

PAUL E. ROBINSON

CSS Publishing Company, Inc.
Lima, Ohio

HOPE BENEATH THE SURFACE

Scripture quotations are from the *New Revised Standard Version of the Bible,* copyright 1989, by the Division of Christian Education of the National Council of the Churches of Christ in the USA. Used by permission.

Scripture quotations are from the *Revised Standard Version of the Bible,* copyrighted 1946, 1952 (c), 1971, 1973, by the Division of Christian Education of the National Council of the Churches of Christ in the USA. Used by permission.

Library of Congress Cataloging-in-Publication Data

Robinson, Paul E., 1945-
   Hope beneath the surface : sermons for first lesson, Advent, Christmas, Epiphany : Cycle A / Paul E. Robinson.
      p.   cm.
   ISBN 0-7880-0436-0
   1. Advent sermons. 2. Christmas sermons. 3. Epiphany season—Sermons. 4. Bible. O.T.—Sermons. 5. Sermons, American. I. Title.
BV4254.5.R63   1995
252'.61—dc20
                                      95-13911
                                         CIP

This book is available in the following formats, listed by ISBN:
0-7880-0436-0 Book
0-7880-0437-9 IBM 3 1/2 computer disk
0-7880-0438-7 IBM 3 1/2 book and disk package
0-7880-0439-5 Macintosh computer disk
0-7880-0440-9 Macintosh book and disk package
0-7880-0441-7 IBM 5 1/4 computer disk
0-7880-0442-5 IBM 5 1/4 book and disk package

PRINTED IN U.S.A.

To my father,
the Rev. Stanley C. Robinson,
through whom I first caught the vision of preaching the faith;
To my mother, Mary Margaret;
To my beloved congregations,
Good Shepherd, Riehenring and Wesley Haus,
Bemus Point, Christ Church, Olean, and
Trinity Church, Grand Island,
who have danced the homiletical dance with me
over these challenging and blessed years of Ordained Ministry;
To my office manager, Peggy Schall,
whose patience, kindness and wisdom are daily gifts;
To my children, Andrew and Martha,
and
To my wife Ellie,
whose love and support are nothing less than Divine.

Table Of Contents

Foreword

Paul Robinson has turned to the Common Lectionary to develop a series of uncommon sermons. Focusing on Advent, Christmas, and Epiphany, he has brought into our consciousness the meaning of incarnation. He has drawn poignant illustrations from his own life experiences as well as from great spirits of the past and present.

The use of Old Testament and New Testament biblical narratives and comments gives the sermons the kind of scriptural authority which is needed, though frequently missing, in today's homiletical work. Here one discovers that scripture does not have to be forced, nor is one coerced into text proofing. Rather, there is a naturalness and a relevance in each reference which finds its way into the sermons.

On these pages one encounters the moving image of the holy God with Isaiah in the temple, the powerful call to justice through the thundering voice of Amos, the depth of despair in the heart of Jeremiah, and the struggle for faithfulness in the prophetic work of Hosea, Elijah, and others.

Underlying every page is the presence of Jesus of Nazareth, who is constantly uppermost as each sermon unfolds. Robinson's writing, like his preaching, reveals a person who is in close touch with the common ventures of life. More significantly, he is in touch with the common people of the working, playing, and suffering worlds. And he is in touch with the eternal verities of the Christian faith.

Written sermons frequently accomplish two distinct purposes. When well written they serve as inspiration, instruction, and spiritual guidance for the reader. They also provide guidelines, or models, for preachers who are engaged in writing sermons. These sermons accomplish both of these tasks.

Every reader who seeks spiritual guidance will be lifted and strengthened by reading these 17 sermons. Each one provides insights and help for Christians who are engaged in the daily struggles of life and death.

Although they do not adhere slavishly to a rigid structure, they will instruct the observant preacher in ways his or her sermons may be crafted. Each sermon is introduced with a clear, concise, and thought-catching statement. For example, "I remember a song some years back that I never liked ..." or "Everyone knows the experience of dragging out of bed on a dark morning in January ..."

Having caught the attention of the reader or listener, the preacher goes on to state a problem, pose a question, or announce a theme. This is all done in two or three very brief paragraphs. Such a technique opens the door for a series of observations, all of them punctuated with biblical insights. Frequently these insights are named, numbered, or otherwise identified. And then the sermon is ended quickly and dramatically with an appropriate verse, hymn quotation, saying of Jesus, or other clinching conclusion.

Young preachers may be instructed and seasoned pulpiteers will find help as they revisit their own homiletical styles.

Of course, not all readers are preachers in search of a tutor. Many persons read sermons because they find help for daily life. These sermons provide not only insights into the fine art of preaching, but help for the fine art of living.

The Rev. Vernon Bigler
Retired United Methodist Pastor
Buffalo, New York

Introduction

I still vividly remember my daughter, Martha, way back in elementary school, working diligently on her book. It was a picture book she wrote for a national contest. She wrote the text, called it *The Rainbow Room*, and did the most exotic and creative color pictures one could imagine. She even bound it like a real book. We were all certain she would win the contest, get the book published, and take us along on the honorary trip to the Midwest for her autograph session in some mega-mall.

It didn't happen. Instead, she got that dreaded letter: "Dear Martha, your book was wonderful, but ..." Eventually the treasured book came home like a prodigal daughter, in a worn envelope we had last seen looking crisp and neatly wrapped with tape and hope. But Martha survived and so did we. We're now trying to locate it somewhere among boxes and drawers, having moved not long ago from Olean to Grand Island, New York.

I said she survived. She did, but partially because of our expert parental guidance. We told her such things as, "It was worth doing, Martha, even though you didn't win," and "You certainly learned a lot in the process, didn't you?" She nodded, as children always do when their parents try to cover up their own disappointment by spouting eternal verities to the kids.

Even way back then I wondered what it would be like for me to write a book. And then a year and a half ago the letter came asking me to produce a book of sermons on the lectionary for Cycle A, First Lesson, Advent, Christmas and Epiphany for the Revised Common lectionary. I don't know whether a book of sermons counts as a *real* book, but I did it and here it is.

It should be noted that my daughter's early book and mine have some distinct similarities, as well as some real differences.

For example, this is also *my* first book and I, too, have learned a lot. I, too, worked hard on it yet wonder how my personal creation will be received in wider objective circles. Finally, both authors are children!

But there are also some differences. Mine is typed with a computer; hers was written out longhand. Her focus was a colorful parrot with a special message. My focus is a magnificent God seen through colorful prophets and a saving Son. And sadly, my book has no pictures.

Preaching is a mystery, both the agony and exhilaration of preparation and the amazing event called the delivery. I've never understood either fully, but I never cease to be astounded at God's activity in both.

Paul E. Robinson
Grand Island, New York
August 1994

Reversing The Flow

One of the greatest challenges of life is to stay in touch with reality and hold on to hope at the same time. And let it be said, clearly and unequivocally, that precisely just such a stance describes the committed Christian.

Some would boast of a strong faith, but would build it by ignoring the realities of the world around them. Others see clearly the reality of the world around them and therefore are unable to hold on to faith or hope in God at all. The biblical faith to which you and I are heirs does not require a choice, for it is a faith thoroughly grounded in reality and history, yet, through it all, trusting and hoping in God.

Today we begin a new Church season in a new Church year. Today is the first Sunday of Advent, the first season of the Church year. And in the course of this Church year we move through Advent, Christmastide, Epiphany, Lent, Eastertide, Pentecost and Kingdomtide. All of these seasons are meant to help us remember and celebrate the life of our Lord and the faith by which we live and die.

Advent comes right in the face of a world filled with violence and pain, cynicism and doubt. Advent comes right in the face of a world which right now is in its annual life-or-death buying frenzy which will determine its very economic health, all because of the birth of Jesus of Nazareth. Wow! How grateful the western world must be for Jesus ... In order for us to build a vital faith and be able to hope in God, we cannot ignore this crazy, materialistic and violent world, and we must joyfully spend our lives coming to know God. This describes the life of Jesus, our Lord and Savior. It also describes much of the life of someone else whom we learn about in the scriptures.

The name Jesus means "God is salvation," or "God is our help." And more than seven centuries before Jesus there lived a man named Isaiah, a prophet, whose name means "the salvation of God." Isaiah brought together as did no other prophet the vital duo of reality and hope. I want us to begin to look at that great message today as we step into the sacred, emotional and culturally colored period of Advent, the weeks leading up to our celebration of Jesus' birth, which we call Christmas.

Isaiah's ministry stretched over a period of 40 years, from 742 B.C. to 701 B.C. His father's name was Amoz, not to be confused with the prophet Amos who was active shortly before Isaiah's ministry began. Isaiah was married (8:3) and had two sons, both of whom were given strange, symbolic names. The first was Shearjashub, which means, "A remnant shall return," and the second was Mahershalalhashbaz, which means "The spoil speeds, the prey hastens." And you thought you didn't like **your** name!

Most of what we know about Isaiah we know only by inference from the book of Isaiah. He moved easily among kings and the ruling class. He stated in the beginning of his book that he saw his visions during the days of four kings of Judah: Uzziah, Jotham, Ahaz and Hezekiah (1:1). On the other hand Isaiah was very comfortable talking about rural life and vineyards, so he must have spent some time away from the city as well.

It's also possible that Isaiah was a priest, especially when we note his dramatic call, which came in the temple, right where a priest would stand.

Holy, holy, holy is the Lord of hosts; the whole earth
is full of his glory . . . Whom shall I send and who will
go for us? And [Isaiah] said, "Here am I; send me!"
(Isaiah 6:3, 8)

And God did and Isaiah went. And we can be grateful he did, for his legacy of prophetic words and images is hard to match anywhere in the Bible.

Early on in the book of Isaiah is a beautiful and powerful passage which launches us nicely into the Advent season. It is a section which is matched virtually word for word by a contemporary of Isaiah, the prophet Micah. I'm speaking of Isaiah 2:1-5 and Micah 4:1-4

The context of this portion of Isaiah is probably a time when Assyria was threatening Judah from the east, when Hezekiah was king and the people had the form but no longer the substance of faith. Right in the middle of such fear and breakdown of faith came this stirring image:

It shall come to pass in the latter days that the mountain
of the house of the Lord shall be established as the
highest of the mountains, and shall be raised above the
hills; and all the nations shall flow to it, and many peo-
ples shall come, and say, "Come, let us go up to the
mountain of the Lord, to the house of the God of Jacob;
that he may teach us his ways and that we may walk in
his paths."

For out of Zion shall go forth the law, and the word of
the Lord from Jerusalem. He shall judge between the na-
tions, and shall decide for many peoples; and they shall
beat their swords into plowshares, and their spears into
pruning hooks; nation shall not lift up sword against na-
tion, neither shall they learn war any more.

(Isaiah 2:1-4; Micah 4:1-3 RSV)

In Micah we find this additional verse added on:

> ... *but they shall all sit under their own vines*
> *and under their own fig trees, and no one shall make them*
> *   afraid,*
> *for the mouth of the Lord of hosts has spoken.*
>
> (Micah 4:4)

These beautiful words of hope and trust and peace were written during a time of fear of war and the rattling of armor. It's as though right in the middle of Palestine the people of Judah were moving in one direction, and, somehow, through a force unseen by everyone else, Isaiah, or Micah, or whoever wrote this priceless piece, was moving in another direction. How could it be that one could speak of peace during war? How could one speak of the weak, backsliding people of Jerusalem as being one day "established as the highest of the mountains" with nations flowing to it, not to make war, but to be taught the ways of peace, the ways of God?

Icebergs. What do you think of when you think of icebergs? The *Titanic*, perhaps? Or, if you've been on a cruise in Alaska or have seen it as I have on television, you may picture huge walls of ice on the edge of the sea "calving," that is, giving birth to icebergs as they break off and plunge with a spectacular splash into the ocean.

I read something interesting about icebergs some time ago. I read that if you were to fly over the North Atlantic in a blimp and were to stare at a large pack of icebergs, you would begin to notice something. You would notice that all the small icebergs would be moving in one direction, while the large ones would be moving in another.

Now why do you think that is? It's because surface winds are moving the little icebergs while the enormous ones are directed and moved by ocean currents deep below the surface.

Right in the midst of turmoil and hopelessness, the surface winds of his day, Isaiah was undaunted in his faith. He knew that such things would pass and that the day would come when the mountain of the Lord would be established as the highest of all. He knew that the day would come when, instead of the people of God turning their backs on the Lord who loved them, once again they would be faithful and by their sheer radiance and the power of God, people would flow back up the mountain to be taught the Lord's way of peace.

I stand before you this day to proclaim with the prophets of old that the way of war will one day be known as stupid and ineffective. I stand before you this day with the prophets of every age who have lifted before all nations the vision of beating swords into plows and spears into pruning hooks, so that men and women, boys and girls can sit peacefully under their vine and fig tree, under their maple tree and cactus, under their palm tree and rubber tree, and live in peace and unafraid.

We've had enough influence flowing from the bowels of evil in our society, flowing into our minds and hearts through television and movies, videos and radio, polluting our children and killing our youth and adults. But the flow will not be reversed until you and I fill ourselves with the Spirit of God in Jesus Christ. The flow will not be reversed until you and I are established in the faith. People will not stream to the mountain of God until that mountain has something dramatic and more exciting and hopeful to offer than what's in the valley.

Advent, a time to prepare to receive the King of kings, the Prince of Peace. A time to receive the One who shows us the way to the Lord of life. A time to celebrate the coming of the One who enables us to move with God no matter how the surface winds may blow and the waves may seek to consume us.

Advent, a time to prepare to reconnect ourselves with Jesus, with the depths of our faith, so that the mountain of the Lord can be established as the highest in the land, so that people will no longer stream away from it but rather will stream to it and say, "Come, let us go up to the mountain of the Lord, that the Lord may teach us his ways and that we may walk in his paths."

My friends, it's time to reverse the flow. And it is the power of the Holy Spirit of God which we celebrate in Jesus that will bring it to pass.

Advent 2
Isaiah 11:1-10

Daring To Trust The Roots

There is so much uncertainty in life that most of us look hard and long for as many "sure things" as we can find. A fisherman goes back again and again to that hole that always produces fish and leaves on his line that special lure that always does the trick. The fishing hole and the lure are sure things.

A gardener finds it hard to switch from tried and true varieties of vegetables. Blue Lake or Provider green beans, Silver Queen white corn, Beefsteak tomatoes, Detroit Red beets all have a familiar, solid ring to them for a gardener. They're "sure things" if the weather cooperates. It's hard to try other varieties.

People are looking for sure things today, in gardening, in buying computer software, hand tools or diapers, in signing position players for baseball or football, in buying a business, and yes, even in giving one's heart to a religion.

And you and I know that those sure things don't always turn out the way we hoped. Think back on your own life. Think back on the decisions you made that you thought were good, informed decisions, and then, poof, up went your dream. It was no sure thing at all.

17

Today you and I are looking for security, for stability, for joy.

This has been going on for a long, long time. Approximately 13 centuries before Jesus, the people of Israel were rescued by God through Moses from their forced slavery in Egypt. After 40 years in the wilderness and receiving the ten commandments at Mount Sinai, they finally found themselves in the Promised Land, the land of milk and honey. Before they went over into the land of Palestine, however, they were warned by the Lord through Moses. They were warned of what would happen if, once they were comfortable again and had their beautiful homes, they forgot who had provided them with all their blessings (Deuteronomy 8:11ff).

Over and over again we read in the Bible that, after they had gone over into the Promised Land, Israel did forget, and "... did what was evil in the sight of the Lord" (Judges 2:11-15; 4:1; 6:1). In other words, instead of leaning on the Lord and being faithful to God and praising God, they were drawn to the pagan gods of Baal. These gods were images they could see, and worship of them included sensuous acts they could enjoy in the temple as a part of the pagan religious rituals. Far more fun than just paying annual connectional apportionments! They forgot who it was they were to be serving and who it was who gave them life.

And over the centuries, the Hebrews wavered back and forth in their covenant with God. Around 750 years before Jesus, there was King Uzziah who, initially, "did what was right in the eyes of the Lord" (2 Chronicles 26:4). But listen to this, from 2 Chronicles 26:15-16:

> *And [Uzziah's] fame spread far, for he was marvelously helped, till he was strong. But when he was strong he grew proud, to his destruction, for he was false to the Lord his God ..."*

Strong, proud Uzziah then contracted leprosy, and lived out his life separated from his people, while Jotham, his son, did the governing. Jotham, who sought to be faithful to God, was followed by his anxious son Ahaz who did not. Ahaz tried to buy the favor of Assyria and frantically made altars to every god he knew of, in hopes that one of them might save his hide and his country Judah. Ahaz was followed by Hezekiah, who sought to break Judah's vassal relationship with Assyria and clean out the altars to foreign gods. Back and forth the kings went, while their people lost more and more of their memory and discipline of being in covenant with their God.

And in the midst of these four kings of Judah, in the seventh and eighth centuries before Christ, Isaiah the prophet sought to bring faithfulness and hope to his people and to the kings whose ear he had from 742 to 701 B.C.: Uzziah, Jotham, Ahaz and Hezekiah (cf. Isaiah 1:1).

Now you may not remember the names of these four kings, and you may even forget the prophet Isaiah's name, but I doubt very much that you will be able to forget the image which he used to solidify hope among a people who were frightened by current events, by the concern over foreign affairs and the sin and wickedness within their own lives and country. Hear the words of Isaiah:

> *There shall come forth a shoot from the stump of Jesse,*
> *and a branch shall grow out of his roots. And the Spirit*
> *of the Lord shall rest upon him* ...   (Isaiah 11:1-2a)

And Isaiah went on to tell of the kind of ruler he foresaw coming from that great stump. And while Isaiah was speaking about an actual king in his own day, he was at the same time speaking a word of hope for people in any age. It is quite natural then that seven centuries later, followers of Jesus would see Jesus the Christ in these words. And so it is that this passage has become one of the key passages we read as we await the celebration of Jesus' birth.

A shoot from a stump. This was an easy thing for me to picture after events at our house this past year. You see we had a very thirsty willow tree not far from our house that was sending large masses of roots into the basement and into the sump pump. Reluctantly the decision was made to cut it down.

19

For some reason, a four-foot stump was left, to be cut down later. I didn't think much about the stump until early this fall when it suddenly struck me as I looked out my bedroom window that I could not even see the stump. Growing out of the sides of that stump was a mass of branches, some of them reaching six feet into the air! It all started with a shoot out of the stump of a willow tree. What a great picture of Isaiah 11:1: "There shall come forth a shoot from the stump of Jesse ..."

So who's Jesse? Jesse was the son of Obed and the grandson of Boaz, the husband of Ruth. Going the other way, Jesse was the father of eight sons and two daughters. And most importantly, one of those sons was David, King David.

In other words, from the heritage of King David, from David's great line, David who sinned yet was used of God for great things, from this heritage that goes back to those who made a great covenant of faithfulness with their God, would come forth a leader. And this leader would be wise, he would not jump to conclusions about issues or about the poor, and he would not weaken before wickedness.

And out of this leadership would come forth a peace in all the earth, even including the natural world, which would be as never before, "... the calf and the lion and the fatling [would lie down together] and a little child shall lead them" (Isaiah 11:6).

Isn't it true that just to hear those lines of Isaiah is to picture rolling eyes and "Get real!" comments from people "in touch" with the realities of the day? Isn't it true that just to allow such grandiose idealism to be seriously verbalized in our modern day is to be shunted aside as Pollyanna, out-of-touch dreamers? Almost as crazy as those who, years ago, held forth hope that one day the Iron Curtain and the Berlin Wall would crumble. A hope that was seen clearly by those praying Christians in the East and radical believers in the West, but derided as nonsense by the clear-thinking "realistic" leaders of the day.

Yet it is true that your and my faith roots go deep into the soil and history of the Hebrew people and our nearer roots in the greatest product of the Hebrew line, Jesus of Nazareth, our Lord and Savior, whose birth we are preparing to celebrate.

And so let us ask ourselves as we move into Advent: Do we trust these roots of ours? Do we trust the roots from which we draw our life?

I wonder if there is not rather a sense that while we should hold on to these roots and connections (and who would openly deny them?), yet do we dare draw primarily from them? I wonder whether in fact we find it hard to allow our hearts to trust that these roots will in time produce the Kingdom of God we talk about, to give us in time the security and meaning and hope of which the scriptures and Jesus are so richly full. Instead, we keep some other roots side-by-side in another part of the garden, roots that go into the soil of rugged individualism, cynical "realism," and hedonistic "get all you can now for tomorrow we die."

Isaiah said, "It's a sure thing." Isaiah said you can trust the roots; you can trust the Lord; in God's timing the Kingdom will come.

I have a garden. One of the new things I have added to it is a bed of strawberries. What a joy it was this past spring to go out to the garden every morning and bring in five or six fresh berries for our cereal! What I have learned, though, is that you mustn't allow the weeds in the strawberry patch to get away from you! I almost allowed that to happen this past spring. So this fall I spent many hours weeding the strawberry bed. I took my long dandelion tool and dug way down deep to get the roots out. And what a mass of roots I found. Virtual sod from grass that had encroached. And those long white roots from crab grass that went everywhere, and the roots of all the little maple trees that were started when the millions of winged seeds covered the land this past spring.

But I also saw some strawberry roots and their runners. And I knew that come spring they would lead to a harvest of strawberries. I was certain. No doubt in my mind.

Such was the faith and hope of Isaiah. You can trust the roots of our faith which spring up out of the heart of God.

Imagine for a moment being able to trust the Gospel; imagine for a moment being able to speak the Word without anxiety and anger, and mean it, that "though the wrong seems oft so strong, God is the ruler yet." Imagine being able to say gently but firmly that out of the stump of Jesse, out of the stump of a Church sometimes gone wrong, out of the stump of a former Christian society that even back then was far from perfect, will come the Kingdom of God.

Imagine being able to say gently but firmly that the life of joy and forgiveness within the Church is a foretaste of things to come and that there will be some in the world who will listen and hear and turn and will be caught up with us in the march to Zion.

Imagine us then no longer anxiously and frantically trying to drag in the Kingdom. Rather it would be up to us to witness to the activity of God today, to point to the divine branches of life through Jesus Christ that even now are growing around the world out of dead-looking stumps, nurtured by roots that are deep in the heart of God.

Isaiah didn't wait around for evidence of hope in order to hope (cf. Romans 8:24-25; Hebrews 11:1). His hope came from a deep and abiding trust in God. And he knew that God would send leaders who would carry on God's message.

You and I have the advantage over Isaiah of knowing the ultimate leader, the ultimate shoot off the stump of Jesse: Jesus Christ. And that branch connects us forever with an undying hope, which is foolishness to the wise and life itself to those who give their life to Him.

Saint Paul wrote in his letter to the church at Rome these words:

> *May the God of hope fill you with all joy and peace in believing, so that you may abound in hope by the power of the Holy Spirit.* (Romans 15:13)

Only through the power of the Holy Spirit are we able to hope in these days. And to that hope I bear witness to you this morning, and to that hope the Church at its best has always borne witness.

You see, it is a sure thing, because we can dare to trust our roots that go deep in the heart of God, roots to which Isaiah pointed, and roots which came to full flower in the face and in the life of Jesus of Nazareth. Thanks be to God!

The Christmas Cactus

Christmas has a way of bringing back memories. One that came to my mind as I was preparing this message was when my family would be driving home at night in the car and my father would lead us in singing a song. To all of us family members who remember those fun, cozy journeys toward home, there are many layers of meaning to the words. The song goes like this:

> *There's a long, long trail awinding,*
> *Into the land of my dreams,*
> *Where the nightingales are singing*
> *And the white moon beams.*
> *There's a long, long night of waiting*
> *Until my dreams all come true,*
> *Till the day when I'll be goin' down*
> *That long, long trail with you.*

I've always found this song, which I understand comes from WWI days, to be a very emotional one for me. I think it's because it deals with the deepest yearnings in everyone's heart. It speaks of seeking after comfort and joy and fulfillment in those deep parts of our being, where we are still children, and where sitting on the lap of an adult in a big stuffed chair is still both possible and desirable.

The journey to the place of our dreams is, of course, a lifelong experience, filled with disappointments, surprises, and enormous challenge.

I have a bias which I will admit to you right up front. I believe that everyone's journey, everyone's drive and yearning, is to be fully connected with the One who created him or her. The drives for success, for money, for power, for a "high," for comfort, for security, whether we realize it or not, are attempted replacements of the basic need to be connected with God. Unfortunately many people have bought into the lie that the hunger they feel can be sated by something else, a substitute, like money or sex or a hot car or a good movie or a new job.

We are all on a journey. And it is a very "long, long trail awinding" indeed, into the land of our hopes and dreams, into the arms of our loving God. Such a journey has been known by people as long as there have been people, for God placed that desire for relationship with God in our very soul. This is what Christmas is all about.

For the people in the day of Isaiah the prophet, 740 years before Jesus was born, their understanding of God was still a mixed message, all jumbled up with their hopes and dreams of deliverance and redemption as a nation. The Jews were a people who had known occupation and threat thereof, a people who knew great kings and leaders as well as weak ones who were unfaithful to God.

For the Jews, the people of Judah, to whom Isaiah was speaking, Zion was always the "land of their dreams." Zion, a word we hear in hymns and scripture, came to mean, over the centuries, the place where one could meet God. Specifically it is a rock outcropping near Jerusalem, now covered by the mosque of Omar. This rock traditionally was the site where Abraham nearly sacrificed his son Isaac. In time the entire City of David, Jerusalem, came to be known as Zion, the City of God. Only later were the Jews to learn that God was to be found everywhere.

Isaiah anticipated the time when, due to their moral and spiritual collapse, they would be conquered by the Babylonians and exiled to Babylon to the east. That finally happened around 600 B.C. Their only hope and every prayer during their 50 plus years of exile was to return to Zion, Jerusalem, the place where their God dwelt. Until then they had to live in Babylon, a pagan land, where people laughed at their faith.

Remember these words of the Psalmist written in the days of their exile?

> *By the waters of Babylon, there we sat down and wept, when we remembered Zion. On the willows there we hung up our lyres. For there our captors required of us songs, and our tormentors, mirth, saying, "Sing us one of the songs of Zion!" How shall we sing the Lord's song in a foreign land?* (Psalm 137:1-4 RSV)

To these people Isaiah wrote the words of the 35th chapter, to a people wishing to go home, wishing for a way back through the long, long trail awinding through scary and barren land, to the land of Zion, the land of their dreams, where they could meet God. What they were to learn was that they needed to take that journey back in their hearts even more than they needed to return bodily.

Is it not true that we are not far from being such a people? We are wanderers in a land that cares little for the holy and worships the idols of wealth and power. We are people who have been baptized as disciples of Jesus, one who came to live before us the radical new life which puts God before money and power, and others before ourselves. It's no wonder King Herod tried to kill the baby Jesus in Bethlehem. He was going to ruin everything!

I heard recently about a meeting of church leaders gathered to talk about major issues of the day. At one point someone suggested that, in order to properly celebrate Christmas, we

27

should spend a minimal amount on presents and focus on the real meaning of Christmas. At this suggestion an irate man stood up and said, "What are you trying to do, ruin the economy and put people out of work? You call that Christian?"

We are on a journey. We are on a journey to Zion, to meet God. We are on a journey to the land of our dreams, some of them understood and clear, and others vague and only a deep longing for something more.

Such was the state of affairs in the world when "the fullness of time came," and a woman was overshadowed by the Holy Spirit, and Jesus was born. In the midst of darkness and despair and a religion heavy with oughts and shoulds and unbearable burdens of countless rituals to get right with God, came Jesus. In the midst of a land where religion was dust in the mouth to many, so much so that many had given up trying, there came an understanding of God's love.

In the midst of a time when people were in a religious desert, where they thought they had to earn the love of an angry, far off God through rituals and sacrifices, came Emmanuel, "God with us," who taught that God already loved them with an everlasting love, and called them to love God, their neighbor and themselves as a response to that love. There came streams of water in their religious desert.

Isaiah wrote to exiles who wanted to go home to Zion, thinking that that was the only way to get close to God. Do you think that you need to be in some other place or circumstance in order to get close to God, in order to continue the journey? Would you like to inhabit some other desert, any other desert than your own?

I was touched by a quote from Scott Russell Sanders:

> *... to withhold yourself from where you are is to be cut off from communion with the source. It has taken me half a lifetime of searching to realize that the likeliest path to the ultimate ground leads through my local ground.*
> (*Context,* November 1, 1993)

It was "local ground" that produced Mary and Joseph; it was local ground that produced Jesus; and it is the local ground where God is at work in your life and mine, bringing streams of living water flowing into our desert spots on our life's journey.

An ornithologist once pointed out that there are two kinds of birds flying over our deserts. There are the hummingbirds and the vultures. The vultures only see rotting flesh, because that's all they look for, and they thrive on it. But hummingbirds pay no attention to dead animals. Instead they look for tiny blossoms and cactus flowers. Each bird finds what it's looking for.

Is it possible that there are some flowers in the midst of the pain in your life that are left untouched by your gaze, whose nectar is waiting to refresh you, a gift of God, manna from heaven?

There's an amazing parallel to Isaiah's 35th chapter, in the 84th Psalm, verses 5 and 6.

> *Happy are those whose strength is in you, in whose heart are the highways to Zion. As they go through the valley of Baca they make it a place of springs; the early rain also covers it with pools.*

Isaiah writes of the highway to Zion, to the land of their dreams, where God is no longer distant, a highway which shall be called the Holy Way.

The Psalmist writes, "Happy are those whose strength is in [God], in whose heart are the highways to Zion."

Do you hear that? "In whose heart are the highways to Zion." No matter what the outward circumstances may be, no matter the desert dust and heat and wind, the journey to Zion is made in the heart. The local circumstances make up the territory, but they are not the highway to God. The highway is in the heart. The long, long trail is in the heart, where neither winning the lottery or losing the winning ticket in the trash makes up the road surface, though it may be a dramatic part of the scenery.

Some of you must have a Christmas cactus. What a gorgeous plant that is. Dainty, bright red blossoms sprouting out on the end of the dark green flat leaves. It was right in the midst of the desert of political unrest, poverty, and religious cynicism that God sent Jesus to live and to be a blossom of hope and truth, the means of connecting us once and for all with our Creator, who loves us more than we can possibly know.

God is always doing such things for us as we traverse the long, long trail awinding into the land of our dreams. No matter the desert through which your life's journey may be taking you this Christmas, no matter the scenery, take to the highway of God. It is that Holy Way in your heart, whose presence Isaiah foretold and whose reality God revealed in a manger, on a cross and in an empty tomb. It is a pool of water in the desert; it is the blossom on the desert cactus; it is the Way, the truth and the life.

It's what really makes it ... a Merry Christmas.

The Christmas Sign

Ever need a sign of hope? Ever need a sign that things are going to be all right? Ever need a sign that you were going to pass the test, or that she wasn't going to break up with you? Ever need a sign that God was still around or that life was still worth living?

Ah, we all know of the need of a sign, don't we? It's funny how we are built. Inside, I mean. We can have proofs and explanations and insistent documentation, but that's not what we really need deep inside, is it? We want a sign.

The most subtle, fragile, subjective hint of all, a sign, is what we need to assure us of our place in a person's life, or to assure us that it'll be okay, or to assure us that God is there.

Just a sign. Like looking off to the side of the cluster of stars called Pleiades to bring them out in a brightness and richness that looking straight on never can do. We often need a subtle but honest sign, a hint of truth from an unguarded moment. A sign.

Centuries before a tiny urgent cry in a bed of hay that night, a king shook from fright at the collaboration of foreign nations who would do Judah in. King Ahaz needed a sign desperately and Isaiah the prophet was sent by the Lord to assure

31

him. "Don't be afraid of these two smoldering stumps of fire-brands," Isaiah quoted the Lord to Ahaz. And then he finished with those marvelous words: "If you do not stand firm in faith, you shall not stand at all."

But they were strong words. They were words meant to convince. They were too direct, too positive for Ahaz to hear. He needed a sign. Just a gentle, subtle sign.

And so, reading his mind, the Lord spoke to him and said, "All right, ask for a sign, any sign! Let it be as high as the sky or as deep as the earth. Just ask me and I'll give it to you."

But Ahaz couldn't do it. The reason he gave was a clear example of false deference to the Lord. "Oh, I couldn't!" More likely it just wouldn't be the same to ask for a particular sign. That would be like having your parents ask you what gift they should surprise you with on Christmas morning! If you tell them, it takes away the surprise!

I can remember the three of us boys as children, sneaking downstairs at 6:30 on Christmas morning. The tree was dark until we plugged in the lights, splashing the wrapping paper with even more color. The presents were all there, and we quietly poked around the pile, trying to guess what might be in the presents with our name on the tag. And after all that effort to guess, what a crushing thing it was when a shape or a rattle or a poor wrapping job enabled us to guess for sure! The fun was gone.

But God was not going to leave Ahaz without his sign, whether he wanted it or not, and so a sign he got. A woman would conceive and bear a son and the name of that son would be Emmanuel. Emmanuel. It means "God with us."

Oh, what a sign. Not a direct statement that God would see to it that the foreigners would not conquer. Not a rosy picture of how the history of the battle would be written. No, it was much more important than that. It was a sign. A gentle, general, generic surprise. We're talking about a king shaking from fear of a foreign army, wondering whether he or the nation of Judah would survive, and the Lord, in spite of his protest, offers ... a sign. God would be there no matter what happened. It'll be all right.

"And this will be a sign for you. You will find the Babe wrapped in swaddling cloths and lying in a manger."

Now that's a more definitive sign, isn't it? I mean, a baby wrapped up in the Pampers of the day. That's not a hint; that's direct, right? Right? Or is it?

Could those shepherds have had a clue as to what was wrapped in those swaddling cloths? Could they have had a clue what was going on in that humble setting where mother shook from the cold and shock of childbirth and father, exhausted from seeking shelter, looked warily out of the stable, not eager to welcome anyone else into their family . . . one more was fully enough for the time being.

Mary and Joseph, too, were looking for a sign. A sign that what they had experienced over the last nine months really was something of God. A sign that they would not be left alone to deal with this. A sign that Emmanuel, God, was with them. Everything had been so powerful that day for them. Only a subtle wisp of a sign would get through to their pounding hearts. Perhaps a little baaa from a lamb did it. Maybe. But surely the Lord gave them a sign of comfort that night.

Christmas is a magic time of signs, most of which are far beyond and beneath words.

One of those magic signs happened at the turn of the century in New York City. The great playwright Moss Hart wrote in his autobiography about a particular Christmas Eve when he was ten. He knew his family was almost penniless, so he was surprised that special night when his father said to him, "Let's go downtown," and they set out on a walk down to 149th Street, a part of town where pushcarts full of toys were lined up for late Christmas shoppers.

Mr. Hart knew his dad was going to buy him a Christmas present, but he also knew that his dad had very little money. As they walked by these carts, Hart said he saw all sorts of toys he wanted. But after his father asked the price, the two of them would move quietly to the next cart, his father putting his hands in his pocket and fingering the coins. So it went from one cart to the other. Nothing the youngster wanted could be purchased for what his father had been able to save. This is how Moss Hart remembered his feelings that night:

> *As I looked up at [my father] I saw a look of despair and disappointment in his eyes that brought me closer to him than I had ever been in my life. I wanted to throw my arms around him and say, "It doesn't matter ... I understand ... this is better than a chemistry set or a printing press ... I love you!" But instead we stood shivering beside each other for a moment, then turned away from the last two pushcarts and started silently back home.* (Homiletics, Oct.-Dec., 1991, p. 42)

A sign had been given. Indirect. But powerful. And a sign had been received.

The question this Christmas is whether we got the Christmas sign. Whether, in spite of or through the plays and the carols, the worship and the family meals, we caught the sign. Whether in spite of missing a family member at the table due to death or distance we saw the sign, the subtle, powerful sign of Emmanuel, God is with us.

If we did, everything else is fine print. If we didn't, then it's back to the war games of Ahaz and back to the filthy sheep on the hillside, with nothing to show for it but a sign. Just a sign.

The Right Child

"A word fitly spoken is like apples of gold in a setting of silver" (Proverbs 25:11). John, the gospel writer, puts it this way: "In the beginning was the Word, and the Word was with God, and the Word was God ..."

These verses of scripture speak of the power and beauty in rightly-chosen words, and therefore speak of these incomparable words from the ninth chapter of Isaiah, the text for this Holy evening, Christmas Eve.

Isaiah tried again and again to express the stubborn hope and dream of *shalom,* peace, which is at the heart of God. "A shoot shall come out from the stump of Jesse ..." (Isaiah 11:1-2). "... and they shall beat their swords into plowshares and their spears into pruning hooks" (Isaiah 2: 2, 4).

Ah, just words they are. Just words. Yet, we read, "In the beginning was the Word ... and nothing that came into being came into being without the Word."

Listen to these words. *Listen* to these words:

> *The people who walked in darkness have seen*
> *a great light; those who lived in a land*
> *of deep darkness, on them light has shined ...*

For to us a child is born, to us a son is given;
And the authority rests upon his shoulders;
  and he is named Wonderful Counselor,
    Mighty God, Everlasting Father, Prince of Peace.
His authority shall grow continually,
and there shall be endless peace for the
throne of David and his kingdom.
He will establish and uphold it with justice and
with righteousness from this time onward
and forevermore.
The zeal of the Lord of hosts will do this.

These are just words, but they are words that have a divine power within them that calls forth that of which they speak. The fact that this kingdom is still so far from our sight diminishes not a whit the truth and the power of this prophetic symphony bequeathed to us by Isaiah.

Some of you are surely familiar with the marvelous musical by O. Henry titled, *The Gift of the Magi.* What a story. In their desperate desire to give a gift to each other on Christmas he sells his watch to buy her a gold hair piece for her lovely, long hair, and she sells her hair to buy him a chain for his gold watch.

One of the highlights of the musical is the song he sings to her when he arrives home and finds her missing her long locks of hair. He sings "Your hair is gone." You simply have to hear it and see it to appreciate it, but the song consists of the rapid repetition of those four words: "Your hair is gone. Your hair is gone. Your hair is gone. Your hair is gone. Your hair is gone. Your hair is gone. Your hair is gone. Your hair is gone. Your hair is gone." The point is made. The shock is fully communicated.

Someone should write a song using as the text this sixth verse of the ninth chapter of Isaiah. "A child is born. A child is born. A child is born. A child is born. A child is born. A child is born. A child is born. A child is born. A child is born. A child is born."

Only two chapters earlier, in chapter 7, we read of the sign given to Ahaz, the terrified king. Though he refused to ask for a sign, the Lord gave him one. "Behold a young woman will conceive and bear a son, and his name shall be called Emmanuel, God with us."

And a child was surely born, then, in Isaiah's day, a child who revealed God's presence to the fearful faithless people in that day. If a child had not been born then, the prophecy would not have made enough of an impact to even be remembered. They would have been only words. Yes, a child was born in Isaiah's day.

But, in the grand way in which God is consistently revealed as personal, a Son was born again, centuries later; only this time it was the Messiah, and Isaiah's words were there in the Jewish scripture like a verbal cradle to receive the Lord Jesus, a symphony of words for a manger: "For unto us a child is born, unto us a son is given, and the government shall be upon his shoulders. And his name shall be called Wonderful Counselor, the Mighty God, the Everlasting Father, the Prince of Peace."

The powers of darkness are immense today, as they surely were then, on that night of nights when, if the truth were told, there was no hush when the baby was pushed out by Mary's last strength. The garish laughter and the drunken din of the mob probably drowned out the first cries of that Holy Child who, some 30 years later, would be serenaded on Golgotha by similar sounds.

And in the midst of the world's darkness it is up to each one of us to choose the authority by which we will live in the midst of that darkness. It is up to each one of us to give over our wills to the lord of our choosing. And it can either be a lord who entices and thrills us for this life only, or it can be the King of kings and Lord of lords. Isaiah writes that this child born for peace would have authority on his shoulders. Indeed, he says, the zeal of the Lord of hosts will do the work.

It is not up to us to bring in the kingdom, but it **is** up to us to decide in which kingdom we will invest our lives.

Sister Joan Chittister writes that the ancients tell the story of a great-hearted soul who ran through the city streets

37

crying, "Power, greed, and corruption. Power, greed, and corruption." For a time, at least, the attention of the people was riveted on this single-minded, openhearted person for whom all of life had become focused in one great question. But then everyone went back to work, only slightly hearing, some annoyed. Still, however, the cries continued.

One day a child stepped in front of the wailing figure on a cold and stormy night. "Elder," the child said, "don't you realize that no one is listening to you?" "Of course I do, my child," the Elder answered. "Then why do you shout?" the child insisted, incredulous. "If nothing is changing, your efforts are useless." "Ah, dear child, these efforts are never useless. You see, I do not shout only in order to change them. I shout so that they cannot change me" (*Context,* January 1, 1988).

To which child have we chosen to give our allegiance? The child of Mary and Joseph? The Prince of Peace? The one mocked by the crowd? Or the handsome child of this world, easy going, well liked, and at home in the power and materialism which is the matrix of our life today? It's important on this Holy Night that in our wandering about from hostel to hostel we pick the right child.

"In the beginning was the Word, and the Word was with God and the Word was God." "For unto us a child is born, unto us, a son is given."

It's the right One. It's the right child.

Divine Naiveté

If you ask a child for his favorite Christmas carol, you'd better be ready! He just might say, "Santa Claus Is Coming To Town." Well, you do know it, don't you?

> *You'd better watch out, you'd better not cry*
> *Better not pout I'm telling you why:*
> *Santa Claus is coming to town.*
> *He's making a list, checking it twice,*
> *Gonna find out who's naughty or nice*
> *Santa Claus is coming to town.*
> *He knows when you've been sleepin'*
> *He knows when you're awake*
> *He knows when you've been bad or good*
> *So be good for goodness sake.*
> *Oh, you'd better watch out, you'd better not cry,*
> *Better not pout I'm telling you why:*
> *Santa Claus is coming to town.*

Some Christmas carol, right? Does anyone disagree with the fact that there are some secular songs which have snuck into our Christmas carol repertoire which only too accurately reflect the secular contamination of the Christian faith?

"Santa Claus Is Coming To Town" is just one. I'll mention another in a moment.

Today is the first Sunday after Christmas and the last Sunday in the year. All of these are good reasons to clear our minds of at least one contaminant which is polluting our holy Gospel.

We have been plumbing the depths of the rich book of Isaiah the prophet and today I want us to look at chapter 63. One of the characteristics of Isaiah, as well as other prophetic literature of the Old Testament, is that on the one hand God is quoted as being ready to destroy the people of Israel for their disobedience, and on the other hand God is there to save them and love them.

This is because of the close relationship between God's hatred of evil, no matter who commits it, and God's unending love and forgiveness of those caught up in such evil.

In chapter 63 is a marvelous verse, verse 8: "Surely they are my people, children who will not deal falsely."

Listen to that verse! Just listen to it. "Surely they are my people, children who will not deal falsely." After centuries and centuries of idolatry and unfaithfulness, after centuries of turning their backs on anything holy, after centuries of going through the motions of religion without carrying it out in their lives ... after all that, the holy God, who knows all, sees all, from whom nothing escapes notice, says something like this, "Surely they are my people, children who will not deal falsely." Who's the Lord trying to kid? Hasn't the Lord checked out recently what the people of God have been up to and into? What an incredible divine naiveté!

I love the story about the man who found his way into church one day for the first time. He had a long police record; he was on drugs and was on a downward spiral. He plopped himself down in the back of the church to see what it was all about.

The theme of the service that day was conversion and forgiveness and the pastor asked people who had stolen things in the course of their lives to stand; then he asked people who had been on drugs and people who were recovering alcoholics

40

to stand. The pastor went on and on listing a whole variety of sins till virtually everyone in the sanctuary was standing. The man in the back told someone later that he thought to himself at that point, "Boy, these are my kind of people!"

After all those members and friends in that congregation were standing, confessing these many and various sins, would their pastor have said to anyone, ". . . these are my people, children who will not deal falsely, people who will not sin"? Of course not. He might truly forgive them and rejoice at their repentance, but he would be, well, naive, to suggest that these folks would not sin. Who could trust his judgment again if he made such a claim, knowing full well that they could not be trusted to walk the straight and narrow?

Compare if you will the difference between our song about wonderful Santa Claus, before whom one must be perfect or tremble, and the Lord God, who embraces imperfect creatures, acting as though they had done nothing wrong.

The parable of the Prodigal Son might better be called the parable of the Loving Father. It was Jesus' way of communicating the amazing love and forgiveness, even apparent naiveté, of a loving father, a God-like father. He surely knew his son would waste his precious inheritance, yet was willing to give it to him, and more amazing still was waiting with open arms to receive him when he came home, destitute, ashamed, and broken.

Don't you see? Don't you hear? The world knows nothing of this. The world only knows of Santa Claus, who doles out gifts to those who are "good."

It's time to sing our second song. I'm sure you know "Rudolph, The Red-nosed Reindeer."

Rudolph, the Red-nosed Reindeer, had a very shiny nose;
And if you ever saw it, you would even say it glows.
All of the other reindeer, used to laugh and call him
    names;
They never let poor Rudolph, join in any reindeer games.
Then one foggy Christmas Eve, Santa came to say:

> *"Rudolph, with your nose so bright, won't you guide my*
>   *sleigh tonight?"*
> *Then all the reindeer loved him, as they shouted out with*
>   *glee:*
> *"Rudolph, the Red-nosed Reindeer, you'll go down*
>   *in history!"*

A man by the name of Bill Kincaid of Ann Arbor, Michigan, had this to say about this song: "Did you know that one of the most morally dangerous and damaging songs is a Christmas tune?" Guess which song he was referring to? You got it: "Rudolph, The Red-nosed Reindeer." Now you probably want to know why. Here is what Mr. Kincaid said:

> *"**Then** the other reindeer loved him," the song says. Not until Rudolph was approved by the authority figure Santa, not until Rudolph had proven that his disability could actually be useful, not until he had done something heroic was Rudolph, with all his differences and disabilities, accepted!*

Quite a thought, isn't it? Love and acceptance in this world tends to be conditional, and the terrible thing around Christmas time is that that ungodly secular tendency has crept into our Christmas songs. You won't find it, though, in our carols. And you won't find it in the heart of God.

Judgment is a part of the divine equation, but we are reminded by Jesus himself that it is not for us to judge (Matthew 7:1f). It is only for us to love. Even the church has gotten into the Santa Claus and Rudolph mentality sometimes. "Look out for the scary God who will get you if you're not good." How different from, for example, Saint Paul's words in Romans, chapter 5:8: "But God proves his love for us in that while we were yet sinners Christ died for us."

God sent us Jesus to express the Lord's amazing divine naiveté, which loves us so much that sins are overlooked enough for us not to get stuck in defensiveness and guilt, so that we might have the heart, the self-esteem, and the motivation to keep trying and keep growing in our walk with the Lord and our neighbor.

Christmas, the birth of Jesus, and the Gospel he came to live and teach is, indeed, good news. It's the result, the fabulous, unbelievable result, of a love beyond our comprehension. A divine naiveté that saves and heals us. Thanks be to God!

Christmas 2
Jeremiah 31:7-14

Satisfaction Guaranteed

I remember a song of some years back that I never liked. The singer screamed as much as he sang, and he repeated the words over and over again. But the message and the title of the song I remember well, and so will you: "I can't get no satisfaction!"

As we think about our lives today, is it not true that there are those days, those weeks, and those periods in our lives when we could easily intone with great feeling, "I can't get no satisfaction"?

My big, red, unabridged power-dictionary I quote now and then defines the verb *satisfy* in this way: to fulfill the desires, expectations, needs, or demands of a person or the mind; to give full contentment to desire, want or need by sufficient or ample provision.

We all know that according to this definition we are not always a satisfied people, who have fulfilled all or even most of the desires, expectations, needs or demands of our hearts. There are at least one or two left unsatisfied, right?

One of the buzz word promises in advertisements today is this: "Satisfaction guaranteed." In fact, this does not say what it seems to say. It does not really say that you will definitely be satisfied with the item. It only means that if you are *not* satisfied, you can get your money back.

With life, it's hard to get your money back if you end up not being satisfied!

We've been looking at the message of the great eighth century B.C. prophet, Isaiah, and we're not done yet. But as a bit of an interlude, as we move into the New Year, I want us to listen to the great prophet Jeremiah. Isaiah received his call from the Lord "the year that King Uzziah died" (Isaiah 6:1ff), which was in 740 B.C. Isaiah responded immediately when God called. "And who shall I send, and who will go for us?" Remember Isaiah's response? "Here I am. Send me."

Isn't it great that God uses every kind of person? God called Jeremiah, too, more than a hundred years later, in 626 B.C. in the thirteenth year of the reign of Josiah, not to be confused with Uzziah. Jeremiah's response to his call, though, was a bit different. When the Lord said, "And who shall go for us," Jeremiah, in effect, said, "Not me! No way!"

According to the record in the first chapter of Jeremiah he said,

> *"Ah, Lord God! Truly I do not know how to speak, for I am only a boy." But the Lord said to Jeremiah: "Do not say, 'I am only a boy'; for you shall go to all to whom I send you, and you shall speak whatever I command you. Do not be afraid of them, for I am with you to deliver you, says the Lord."*

And though Jeremiah complained to the Lord, and wished that he had never been born (Jeremiah 20:14), he did finally deliver the message. In fact, the message is even more powerful for us today because of all the insight we receive into the spiritual life of Jeremiah, as he struggled with his relationship with God. Isaiah was strong and undeterred. Jeremiah, on the other hand, was more like you and me, hesitant, resentful at being put out, and easily offended and hurt by the comments of other people.

However, in spite of his hesitance, Jeremiah did some remarkable things in communicating his message of both doom and hope to the people of Israel and Judah. His very life communicated the message of hope in the midst of great foreboding in the short run.

William Green, a UCC pastor in Pennsylvania, writes that during a period of time in seventeenth century England, worship was a crime, and thousands of churches were torn down. One church was built, though, right during those terrible times, a church which still stands, with the following inscription on its door:

> *In the year 1653 when all things sacred throughout the nation were either demolished or profaned, Sir Robert Shirley . . . founded this church whose singular praise it is to have done the best things in the worst times and hoped them in the most calamitous.*

This is the kind of thing Jeremiah did. He went out and purchased land on which to build a house someday, right when his country was about to be overthrown by the Babylonians (cf. Jeremiah 32). Hope in the midst of despair.

And in the portion of his prophecy we heard this morning, Jeremiah foresaw his people restored to their homeland. And even more importantly, he saw them "radiant over the goodness of the Lord," and "satisfied with [the Lord's] bounty."

My goodness but it takes a lot to satisfy us, doesn't it? I was talking to a friend this past week who told me of her Christmas morning gift-giving experience this year. In her family all the presents for each person are taken from beneath the tree and placed before them. Then they are opened one by one, each person taking a turn. One of her nieces, after her five presents were placed on her lap, said in that special whiny voice, "Is this all I get?"

It takes a lot for us to be satisfied today. What a wonderful prophecy, what a wonderful dream it is, that one day we might actually be satisfied, radiant over the goodness of the Lord, irrespective of how much money we have or presents we get.

I will repeat what I have said before. I believe that all of our longings have at their center a longing for relationship with God. That is our basic hunger. Unfortunately many people perceive that longing as a longing for something else, for things, for toys, for sex, for money, for adventure, for power, for food. I believe that all those drives for things are put in their proper place when the longing for relationship with God is satisfied.

Remember that conversation Jesus had with his disciples which John reported in chapter 14? Philip said a mouthful in the course of that conversation. In verse 8 we read: "Philip said to [Jesus], 'Lord, show us the Father, and we will be satisfied.' " That's true, and he did and they were and we can be, too.

The coming year holds a lot in store for all of us. We don't know what's coming, but we know that God will be with us when it does. Jesus was clear about that. Jesus assured us that the Holy Spirit, the Comforter, would be with us always (John 14:25f). If we are focused on coming to know God through Jesus Christ and the Holy Spirit, daily praising God for the bounty around us, even on our worst days, then we will find ourselves, "radiant over the goodness of the Lord."

If we daily give thanks to God for the gift of life and hope and eternal life, even in the midst of the incredibly difficult challenges in our lives, then we will be satisfied, for we will be consciously in the presence of God. If we try any other way of life we will be sent reeling in times of trouble and heartache.

A Frank Harrington tells the story of a mountain climber who, after years of dreaming and planning and training, climbed the great Matterhorn, that uniquely shaped mountain in southeastern Switzerland. The man and his guide finally made it to the summit, with the raging wind blowing against them. Exhilarated at the incredible view and having reached the top, the man started to stand up and take it all in.

Fortunately, the guide was alert and grabbed him before he did so, screaming in his ear above the raging gale, "Stay on your knees, man, or the winds will blow you off the mountain!"

Indeed they will. So let's stay on our knees this year, in touch with the God we know in Jesus. For with God, satisfaction is guaranteed.

Epiphany Of The Lord
Isaiah 60:1-6

A Most Important Dawning

Early in January in northern Canada the sun peeks above the horizon for the first time after six weeks of hiding. An important dawn for Canada. Imagine how the lives of people in the northern latitudes would be different if they got used to the darkness and never even expected that a dawn would ever lighten their horizon again.

The people to whom the prophets Isaiah and Jeremiah witnessed and preached so long ago were a people whose hope for dawn had been all but extinguished. First the northern kingdom, Israel, had been conquered by Assyria and sent into exile in 721 B.C., and then the southern kingdom, Judah, was conquered by the Babylonians in 587 B.C., and exiled to Babylon, hundreds of miles to the east.

A generation of Jews then lived with waning hope of ever seeing their homeland again, of ever walking through the gates of Jerusalem again, of ever stepping onto the porch of Zion, the temple of God, again.

In 539 B.C., however, Cyrus, the leader of the Persian Empire, conquered the Babylonians, and in 538 B.C. decreed that the Jews should be allowed to go home (Ezra 1:2-4; 6:3-5). The experience was overwhelming, exhilarating.

What was important just prior to this, though, was the vision of the prophets Isaiah and Jeremiah, who, right in the midst of the worst of times, kept the vision of God's mercy and forgiveness alive. They predicted that the time would come when God would move the hearts and wills of appropriate leaders, and the exiles, the captives, would go home again to Jerusalem and Zion, the Mount of God.

In chapter 60 of Isaiah, which we are looking at today, Isaiah paints a dramatic picture of the future, when the Jews would rebuild their razed city and rise up with new energy and purpose. At the same time other nations, inspired by the dramatic reversal in their fortunes and impressed with their powerful God, would send gifts of homage to this great King of kings. Bronze and iron and gold and silver all would pour in (Isaiah 60:17). It would arrive by camels from the east and stream in on ships from the west, all the things necessary to rebuild Jerusalem and the Temple.

Today is the first Sunday of Epiphany, the first Sunday after January 6, which is Epiphany Day. The word *Epiphany* means "manifestation," or revealing. It is when we celebrate the time that the rest of the world comes to see the bright hope and good news of God's Son, Jesus Christ.

In our tradition, the story which exemplifies this moment is that of the wise men who came from the pagan East. There are three gifts, gold, frankincense and myrrh, so we have traditionally thought of three wise men, though the scriptures don't tell us how many there were.

You can see how similar this epiphany celebration is to the prophetic vision Isaiah paints of nations coming in homage to Jerusalem when the exiles are allowed to return home. We're talking here about the world's recognition of the glory of the Lord.

I'd like us to think about that for a moment: the recognition of the glory of the Lord. We've heard songs such as, "You are worthy." We remember the song of the angels as the shepherds were told of Jesus' birth, "Glory to God in the highest."

Think for a moment. Have you recognized the glory of God? And has it dawned on you the importance of God's revelation through Jesus of what God is really like?

Many things in our life take quite a while to really get through. We hear something and think, "Yeah, that's right, I guess." Then we see its truth again and we think, "Oh, yeah, that really is true." And then, after perhaps many moments of casual insight we finally say, with full conviction, "Oh, **now** I understand!!"

Years ago someone told me about their little boy who was told not to go into the street because he might get hit by a car. Time and again he went into the street anyway, and time and again he was punished for doing so. He just didn't get it.

Then one day the family was riding in the car and there was a dog, dead in the middle of the road. The little boy seemed to be deep in thought for a moment and finally said, "Oh, is **that** why you don't want me to go into the road?"

Think for a moment. Have you recognized the glory of God? And has it dawned on you the importance of Jesus' revelation of who God is and what our relationship to God and to one another is designed to be?

You know the "new Christian" temperament? It describes how someone acts who has just learned about God's love in Jesus Christ. The person is excited, and glowing with relief and joy. The burden of years of trying to get right with God and with everyone else has been dropped at the foot of the cross, and the relief and gratitude are overwhelming.

How long has it been since you have known the "new Christian" feeling? Have we forgotten the lifesaving Good News Jesus came to bring?

Isaiah spoke of whole nations streaming to Zion with gifts to this great God. The wise men brought gifts to the King of kings and Lord of lords. Nicodemus learned that nothing less than being "born again" was needed in order to get out of the humdrum, dull, boring, depressing religious life people knew in his day.

Dr. Leonard Sweet, president of United Theological Seminary in Dayton, Ohio, mentions in his book *Quantum Spirituality* something that sports journalist George Plimpton had written. Mr. Plimpton had written about a "mysterious component" in an athlete's life. He said that when this component is added to an athlete's natural ability, it gives a player "a kind of boost, like an afterburner kicking in, a psychic energy that makes the whole greater than the sum of its parts." He called it the "X Factor" and called it a combination of "adrenaline, intelligence, confidence, concentration, and discipline."

The "X Factor." Dr. Sweet then went on himself to say this:

> *For Christians the difference between an ordinary community and an extraordinary, life-producing organism is one word: Christ. Christ is the "X Factor," the "Inner Power" that transforms an assemblage of individuals into a synergic [sic] community of healing and love.*
> (From *Quantum Spirituality*, p. 137)

A synergetic community of healing and love is one in which everyone is working together cooperatively with God and with one another. This happens through the Spirit of Christ revealed to us by our loving God.

Have we forgotten the X Factor in our lives? Have we failed to keep up front in our minds and hearts the total life-changing power of God's love and life as revealed to us in Jesus of Nazareth? Have we gotten sucked into the worst of the institutional church that keeps us busy doing good things, and forgotten the best of the church, its very purpose, which is bringing salvation and hope and joy and new life specifically through God's love known in Jesus, and then offering it to all the world?

Oh, God help us if that has happened! Oh, what darkness if that has happened! Oh, how God's Spirit must be grieved if that has happened to even one of God's children!

It could be the most important dawning in your whole life; it could be a dawning that has never yet occurred to you, to recognize the incredibly wonderful, life-changing power unleashed by God, through the gift of Jesus. The fact that many in the church have domesticated that gift, used it for their own purposes, and turned it into a business or another fine, upstanding club does not take away the truth. The fact that we, day after day, go through religious motions and fail to reach out to the Lord at our side, does not remove the Lord's presence there.

Thomas H. Troeger once said this: "To undomesticate God, to see God in places where we are convinced God would never be, is to be able to hope and believe again."

Isaiah saw into the future when it would dawn on the nations how great was the God of the Hebrews. And when it dawned on them, they would not keep themselves from pouring out their praise and presents in adoration and worship.

The wise men knew that this was the King of kings when Jesus was born, and they could not but search for him, crossing a dangerous desert to find him and worship him. It dawned on them, and they responded. Has it dawned on us yet?

Elizabeth Barrett Browning wrote these marvelous words:

> Earth's crammed with heaven,
> And every common bush afire with God;
> But only he who sees takes off his shoes;
> The rest sit round it and pluck blackberries.
> *Aurora Leigh,* Book VII

I tried so hard not to tell the following joke, but it simply would not keep itself off the computer screen. For those of you who have heard it often, forgive me. It's the story of the man who went into the hardware store in need of a chain saw. He was finally sold on one after being told he could cut up 10 cords of wood a day with it. Excited and eager to get started he took it home and got to work.

After several days, however, the man was really discouraged. The best he could do was half a cord a day, and even doing that was an utterly exhausting experience. Discouraged, disappointed, and not a little angry, he went back to the hardware store with his chain saw, plopping it up on the counter. "So, how's it going, Frank?" the store owner said.

"Look, my good friend, you told me I could cut 10 cords of wood a day with this [expletive deleted] thing. The best I can do is half a cord and even at that it's incredibly hard work. I want my money back!"

"Well, Frank, let's just take a look." With that he adjusted the proper switches and gave a yank on the cord. The saw sprang to life, frightening Frank out of his wits. "Hey," he yelled, jumping back in fear, "what's that awful noise?"

My friends, am I wrong in saying that many people have been living by what they call the Christian faith all their lives, yet have never known more than committee work and fund raising, and wonder why the faith means so little to them?

Am I wrong in saying that there are those who wonder why they have to get involved in prayer and Bible study and service to the hurting of the world and then wonder why their life is still empty, even when they go to church?

This week keep in your mind's eye the picture of that man, rubbing that chain saw back and forth across a tree trunk, with a silent motor, scratching and rubbing and sweating and cursing. And then picture the millions of people who have a general belief in a general God who gives us general hints about general situations and invites us to live a generally good life following some general rules from a generally all-around-good-guy, Jesus, who lived 2,000 years ago, or so.

Such a general religiosity does not take away the depression over the personal pain in a person's life. It does not move one to cross deserts and walk through pagan work places and schoolrooms to witness confidently and gently to God's love seen in Jesus. But to really experience that exciting truth, to finally let the significance of the truth of God's present, active love that we know through Jesus light up our days, that would be the most important dawning of our lives.

Epiphany 1
(Baptism Of The Lord)
Isaiah 42:1-9

The Sacred Other

Schindler's List is a movie one doesn't forget. One of the most horrible scenes is that of the commandant who, for his own amusement and in order to watch the prisoners scatter, uses a rifle to shoot some of the Jews in the courtyard of the prison camp.

This one vignette graphically portrays the opposite of the message the prophet Isaiah was communicating in the portion of his writings we are looking at now, chapter 42, verses 1-9. "A bruised reed he will not break." All of us surely shudder and shrink from the unthinkable carnage and lack of any semblance of human decency depicted in that scene from the film, so different from protecting even a bruised reed in the wind. What is so troubling is that our minds and emotions have adjusted themselves only too easily to scenes only too similar to the one in the movie.

How do we find the road back to a mentality and approach to the world and our neighbors which is gentle and treats all life as precious and loved by God? It's a tough job and the way is long and tedious and frustrating, but it is a way disciples of Jesus Christ are called to travel.

Most of us know something about Albert Schweitzer, the German organist turned missionary doctor, who gave his life to the needy people in Africa, received the Nobel Peace Prize in 1952 and died in 1965. If you knew anything at all about Dr. Schweitzer it was probably the fact, whether it was literally true or not, that he would not kill the smallest living thing, even an insect. There are times even today when I will spare the life of a fly or a spider or an ant, specifically because of a thought about Dr. Schweitzer. Instead of squashing the little creature, I'll slip a piece of paper under it or capture it in my hand and put it outside. (That's probably more humane in the summertime than it is in the winter!) If Dr. Schweitzer felt that way about insects, we can imagine how he felt about people.

So what is our attitude supposed to be about other people? The prophet Isaiah often speaks of the Jews as God's servants. Way back in the book of Genesis, chapter 12, we read of God calling Abram, soon to be called Abraham, to step out in faith and go to a new land which God would show to him. And God said Abraham would be blessed by God, but for the purpose that Abraham might be a blessing to others. He was to be God's servant in caring for other nations and peoples of the world.

The prophet Isaiah, whose ministry began 740 years before Jesus lived, often quoted the Lord as calling the people of Israel "God's servant." In chapter 41, right before the chapter we're looking at this morning, we read in verses 8 and 9:

> *But you, Israel, my servant, Jacob, whom I have chosen, the offspring of Abraham, my friend; you whom I took from the ends of the earth, and called from its farthest corners, saying to you, "You are my servant, I have chosen you and not cast you off"; do not fear, for I am with you ...*

It's clear, then, when we come to chapter 42, that the word "servant" refers to the people of Israel, in this case, not the

Messiah who would come to save them and allow them to return to Jerusalem from their exile in Babylon. Even though the servant here is referred to in the singular, it is the whole people of Israel that is meant.

So what will this servant of God be like? What describes the servant of God whom God will uphold? Listen. Here it is, Isaiah 42:2-3:

> *He will not cry or lift up his voice, or make it heard in the street; a bruised reed he will not break, and a dimly burning wick he will not quench; he will faithfully bring forth justice.*

The servant of God, those called by God's name, will not be loud and pushy; they will protect all life, even fragile, insignificant-appearing life, as an act of obedience and love for the Creator of all life.

I will refrain from dumping all that is in my heart on this matter, for it is not necessarily edifying to hear what we all already know. But let me say this much. I long for gentleness in our society. I long for the day when children and youth will not feel free to trash road signs and break windows and dump garbage from their cars. I long for the day when people will not enjoy the sight of people being blown away by machine gun fire and bombs, when withering language and racism and killing will be as unthinkable in our regular movie theaters as full frontal nudity still is, at least for yet a little while.

The Lord said through Isaiah that the servant of the Lord, the people of God, would be a gentle people, a people who would witness to the life-giving desire of God. That's us, folks. How are we at protecting a simple bruised reed, seen by a frozen lake, or at protecting the last gasp of a smoldering candlewick?

I remember well a conversation I had some years ago about this time of year. It was about Martin Luther King, Jr. I guess I had been protected a bit, for it was the first time I had heard members of a church express a total lack of appreciation for the life and ministry of this great prophet of our time. I will admit to being biased. The dean of Wesley Theological Seminary while I was there was L. Harold DeWolf. Dean DeWolf was Dr. King's mentor and friend through his doctoral program and throughout his momentous ministry.

While I always knew Dr. King was not Jesus and was not perfect, I have always respected him as a man who dared to speak truth and face the most violent racism with courage and gentleness. While his heart was frequently broken by those who were known as his followers but did not always follow his nonviolent passion, Dr. King himself stuck to nonviolence as the only way to solve racism or any other problem.

The fact that our country has made so little progress in rooting out racism and violence since his passing is surely the most tragic reality which confronts us as we celebrate Dr. King's life and faith and philosophy of life. As Claude Lewis of the *Philadelphia Inquirer* has written, "Though King is gone, many still believe in his ideas," but the celebration of his life is made far less meaningful by the fact that "the hatred and the killing goes on."

The words of Isaiah ring across the centuries. The ideal is a precious image for us all. It is an image which the Master, Jesus of Nazareth, fully lived out on this earth, "a bruised reed he will not break and a dimly burning wick he will not quench." Such was the life of Jesus. And so we have inherited that Golden Rule that we all have printed on our rulers, and then we use those rulers to slap and bruise! "In everything do to others as you would have them do to you; for this is the law and the prophets" (Matthew 7:12).

God has designed the world to work smoothly only when the needs and feelings of others are held in the same esteem as our own, where the pain of a mere splinter consumes our lives. God's design is for us to see every other person as sacred.

Some time ago I read about a Doug Nichols who was a missionary in India in 1967. He tells of spending several months in a sanitarium with tuberculosis. Being a missionary, he was eager to share the Gospel with the doctors and nurses and patients, but everyone saw him as a rich American and simply would have none of his tracts and well-meaning witness.

One night Mr. Nichols was awakened by his own coughing around 2 a.m. As he was trying to recover from a coughing spell, he noticed an elderly, very sick patient across the aisle trying to get out of bed. He would sit up on the edge of his bed, try to stand, but finally fall back into bed. He remembers hearing him finally start to cry.

The next morning Mr. Nichols found out that the man was simply trying to go to the bathroom, and ended up going in his bed, producing an awful smell throughout the ward. The nurses were upset, and roughly handled him as they cleaned up the mess. The poor man, embarrassed to death, simply curled up and wept.

The next night, Mr. Nichols again was awakened by another coughing spell and noticed the same man going through the same agony. Finally, Mr. Nichols struggled out of bed himself, and carried the dumbfounded man to the toilet, a small room with a simple hole in the floor. When he got back to the man's bed he said something to him that he assumed was "Thank you."

You can guess the rest. From the time the sun came up that next day people were at his bed, asking for his leaflets and reaching out for the Gospel of Christ. All because he took a man to the bathroom. All because he treated him as a sacred child of God.

Even those who do not know Christ are precious in God's eyes and are to be precious in our eyes as well. Only secondarily do we try to change a person. All people are children of God, of sacred worth, who have come to their conclusions about life and faith through varied and challenging meanderings, as have we.

We all take our turns at being bruised reeds and dimly burning wicks, don't we? God cares for us right at those points. And we, as God's people, and surely as disciples of Jesus Christ, are called to go and do likewise. So let's do it.

Epiphany 2
Isaiah 49:1-7

Too Light A Thing

A man by the name of Kevin Trudeau has marketed a memory course called "Mega-Memory." In the beginning of the course he quizzes the participants about their "teachability quotient." He says it consists of two parts. First, on a scale of one to ten "where would you put your motivation to learn?" Most people would put themselves pretty high, say about nine to ten, he says.

Secondly, though, Kevin asks the listeners of the tape to put themselves on a scale of one to ten in terms of his or her willingness to change! Ah hah! Now that's another matter altogether. Many of us want to diet, but we refuse to change our eating habits or begin to exercise. Many of us want to get better grades in school, but we simply are not willing to change the amount of television we watch and the amount of going out on the weekend. We want to be a better learner, but it just won't happen, because we refuse to change.

To give us a bit of summertime in the midst of our cold winter, let me tell you about an incident I remember my father relating in one of his sermons years ago. It was a hot summer night in Mansfield, Pennsylvania. All the windows were open in my parents' bedroom and they heard clearly two women who were walking down North Academy Street. Just as they were passing under the windows of our house the one said to the other, "Well, that's just the way I am and I can't change it!"

In our really honest moments don't we find ourselves often in that same bind? There are so many things we would like to change in ourselves, but, well, we just can't do it. This morning we're talking about a message from Isaiah and the Lord that would require some change in our whole approach to life, both church life and our personal life. Are we open to such change? We'll see . . .

We've been getting to know Isaiah, the son of Amoz. He lived almost eight centuries before Jesus was born. He began his ministry in 740 B.C. He is recognized as the greatest of all the prophets. Isaiah said right in the first verse of the Old Testament book named after him, that he was active during the reigns of kings Uzziah, Jotham, Ahaz and Hezekiah. He called a spade a spade and brought both warning and hope to the people of the southern Kingdom, Judah, in which Jerusalem was located.

In chapter 49 with which we are dealing this morning, the "servant" referred to means the people of Israel, at least those in Israel who still knew themselves as God's servants. The chapter begins with a call to attention:

> Listen to me, O coastlands,
> Pay attention, you peoples from far away!
> The Lord called me before I was born,
> While I was in my mother's womb
> He named me.
> He made my mouth like a sharp sword . . .
> He made me a polished arrow . . .
> And he said to me, "You are my servant . . ."

And as we read in verse 4, this servant of God, the people of Israel, felt discouraged, guilty and ineffective: "I have labored in vain, I have spent my strength for nothing and vanity." Ever feel that way?

So the prophet Isaiah goes on to speak of Israel's persistent trust in God, in spite of their failures. Indeed Israel says in verse 5 ". . . my God has become my strength." One might add, "It is high time!"

We're approaching now the verse that will be our challenge this morning, but are you following the thought here? Discouraged Israel, who saw herself as called to be God's servant since before they even came in to existence, still felt like a failure in being God's servant, though some resilience of faith remained, in that Israel still saw God as her strength.

And now Isaiah quotes the message to God's failed servant Israel:

> *It is too light a thing that you should*
> *only be my servant to your own*
> *struggling people. I now give you*
> *as a light to the nations, that my*
> *salvation may reach to the end of*
> *the earth.*

Do you get it? God's servant, Israel, was called to preach to her own people, and failed in even doing that. God then said in effect, "Hey, it's too little a thing for you to just scurry around among your own people with my message. What I really need you to do is get the message out to the world, to people who haven't a clue of who I am and how much I love them."

"It's too light a thing." What a phrase! It really captures me every time I read it. What a challenge to those of us who call ourselves servants of God. We struggle with little things so long that they fill our lives and become the big things.

Isn't that one of the dangers of retirement? You spend your life wrestling with heavy responsibilities on a job, whether it's in the home with the impossible challenge of raising children, or out in the business world, where the bottom line looms as the be all and end all. And then you retire, and the little things can easily take over. The anxiety about the leak in the roof.

The anger about the neighbor who splashes too much in the pool late at night. The frustration over the social security check that arrived a day late. Little things can take over and fill the available space in the mind and heart.

But followers of Jesus Christ can do the same. We are called to go into all the world and preach the Gospel, but we can end up worrying over whether the attendance is up or down from last year. We can find ourselves consumed over important institutional things, instead of passionately involved in the salvation of God's world, which is the biggest thing. Do we hear God calling?

> "Church, I call you to more than this. It is too light a thing that you aim to pay all your bills. I call you to give away half your income.

> "It is too light a thing that you aim to pay your apportionments. I call you to support the same number of missionaries in the United States and abroad as you have serving in your church office.

> "It is too light a thing that you have 12 people studying the scriptures once a week in your Disciple class on Monday evening. I call you to have an intensive scripture study going every night of the week to counter the violent, cynical, faithless fluff that people are inhaling daily over the airways.

> "It is too light a thing that you have one pastor and a few lay people trying to reach out to the membership of this congregation. I call your pastor to train 100 people who will reach out to thousands in your community and beyond.

> "It is too light a thing ..."   Do you get the idea?

Why do you think it is that a church can typically find it impossible to pay the normal bills, yet is able to organize, plan for and pay for a new building? Most churches would find it difficult to finance an outhouse for mowing equipment, but would have no trouble building a brand new sanctuary. The problem is not finances. The problem is the source of our motivation. And God knows that we respond to grand visions and important ventures for the Lord that make a difference in the world.

I've been going to a physical therapist for the last month or so. I've been learning a lot. I first went for a gimpy knee, then, in doing exercises for that, threw out my back, which has been a problem for me over the last 30 years. And in the process of doing exercises for my back I came to be aware of problems in my neck.

You know what I found out? I found out that I've been doing a number on my body for most of my life through bad posture, and only now are the results beginning to show and take their toll. I'm having to think now about how I stand and how I sit. And I'm told that if I correct those things, I won't have these problems that have plagued me off and on for years. But that means change in my life, change of some very basic things, like posture.

I believe that disciples of Jesus have been plagued for years with doing things that are too light for us. We have enormous muscles, both physical and spiritual, and we haven't used them. We could move mountains and yet we are afraid to try, because we have been stymied for so long by focusing on how to move mole hills.

And that goes for church work and it goes for us personally. God has unlimited resources for us and calls us to reach out to the world with those enormous resources.

In what ways is God calling us away from lightweight things? To what ventures are we being led or called? What about in your own life?

I've always been intrigued by the story, supposed to be true, of a man who was so discouraged by his poor health that he decided to end it all by running until he dropped. So, he got his things in order and one day started to run until he dropped.

He ran and ran and ran and ran, and, while he got exhausted, he didn't "drop." So he decided he'd do it again the next day, but this time he absolutely wouldn't stop until he dropped.

Perhaps you can guess the end of the story. The man ran and ran, pushing himself to his limit instead of pampering himself in an armchair popping pills, and his body became strong and the man had a new life. There is some truth in the story both for an individual and for Christ's church.

The last words Jesus' disciples heard from Jesus, when he ascended into heaven, were these, ". . . you will be my witnesses in Jerusalem, in all Judea and Samaria, and to the ends of the earth."

People say "charity should begin at home," and that is surely correct. Our problem is that so often it ends there. The person or the church with the world view, with the cosmic view, is so filled with compassion for others, that the people close at hand end up being beneficiaries of that same compassion. It doesn't automatically work the other way around.

There are some of you here today who are feeling totally overwhelmed by life right now. I know that. And the issues for some of you are not light ones, they are bona fide heavy ones. Only you know the application in your life of the truth that Isaiah and Jesus were preaching.

All I know is that God is sure to bless with new energy and new options and new vigor and new joy the persons or the church that chooses to dare great things for people beyond themselves, to be, as Isaiah said, "a light to the nations" out of commitment to and gratitude for God's great love for us which we have seen and known in Jesus Christ.

Focusing only on ourselves and on easily reachable goals is simply too light a thing. It leads to un-health, dis-ease, and plugs up the flow of God's Spirit and power, so that even the "easy goals" are found to be unattainable.

What this might mean for you and me and this church might make great dinner conversation, church committee discussion and prayer time contemplation this week. May we be open to what God would speak to us.

Epiphany 3
Isaiah 9:1-4

Adjusting To The Light

Everyone knows the experience of dragging out of bed on a dark morning in January, stepping around the busy humidifier spewing mucous membrane-healing moisture, finding the door to the bathroom and flipping the switch — whoops, no, not that one, as the fan roars prematurely — there, the light switch.

"Ouch!" we say or think, and the photons from Edison's folly crash against the reluctant retinas of our eyes. We are blinded. We have a fleeting bed wish, yet know that the time is nigh, and the pain must be borne, the face confronted, the sleepers removed, the "natural" beauty restored with soap and water, and the variety of applications applied that sometimes are required for troublesome corners of God's creation called "face."

Finally we realize that the squinting has subsided. But then when we return to the bedroom to turn off the belching humidifier, our retina and iris and brain are all put to work again, adjusting now to the absence of light, as they had only recently adjusted to its glaring presence.

This past Monday evening, the Administrative Board looked at a video that told about our Conference Apportionments and what they accomplish. We tried watching it with the lights on but then decided to turn them off, and indeed we were then able to see better. I remember thinking, as the lights went out, how pitch black the room was and how bright the screen was. In just a few moments, however, the room seemed downright lit up, both from the light in the hallway and the light from the television screen. Adjusting to the light; adjusting to the darkness.

Isaiah says in that marvelous ninth chapter words that bring up memories of Christmas Eve services and all that goes with them: "The people who walked in darkness have seen a great light; those who lived in a land of deep darkness — on them light has shined" (9:2).

The prophet Isaiah, who spoke words of challenge and hope to the people of Israel eight centuries before Jesus was born, created a marvelous picture here, a powerful image. It spoke to the people of his day and it speaks to us in our day.

Darkness is a relative thing. Do you suppose that all the people of Israel felt that they were living in darkness? Or had they simply gotten used to the constant threat of foreign armies, the turmoil and meaninglessness of playing the harlot with other gods than the one who had brought them up out of the land of Egypt, the God of Abraham and Sarah and David? Is it possible that there were those who heard these words and said to themselves, "Darkness? What darkness?"

Is that not what our nation has experienced? The joy of the World War II victory, then the Korean War victory, and the economy and standard of living began to crank up. Even churches were booming, people joining as fast as membership classes could be formed.

Who was aware of the darkness? Who noticed the shallow commitment when people joined our booming churches? Who noticed the racism which had become so institutionalized that to the haves it was invisible and to the ethnic minorities it was simply a way of life?

Darkness? What darkness? Sexual promiscuity was hidden but rampant, and married couples endured lifeless marriages, because divorce was too great a taboo to bear. Women had to fight for anything they could get, and men had to be men, strong, stoic, and alone. And congregations worshipped and sang and preachers preached waves and waves of words, but few got wet. Darkness? What darkness?

And today, while divorce for most is a reluctant, painful last resort, for many it is the first resort. Sexual promiscuity is out in the open, women are still fighting for equal recognition and pay, but are now privileged to get the same stress-related diseases as men. Youth have all the stimulation they want through videos and automobiles, and racism continues. And congregations worship and preachers preach and . . . and what?

I'll tell you what. There really are those who are aware of the darkness. And there are those who have seen the great light. But it takes a long time to adjust to the light.

For years preachers preached about banning the bomb. And then, finally, prayers were answered, hearts were touched, and the problem now is what to do with all the plutonium from all of those bombs.

For years the church taught about the destructive power in lives and families of alcohol and drugs, but it was called naive and moralistic. Now it is nationwide news that leaders in schools are pledging with their students to use no drugs of any kind.

For years the church has preached the joys of sex, sex in the bonds of marriage, and people have laughed. Today the word abstinence before marriage is gaining ground, if even in small conclaves.

I believe that a society that has lived in darkness so long finds the light painful, for it has adjusted to the darkness. But over time, by God's grace and the gentle, persistent work of faithful Christians, people see the light, adjust to the light, and lives are changed.

There was a blooper headline seen in a Poughkeepsie newspaper: "Two Persons Hurt In Route 9 Crash — Peekskill Woman Suffers Consciousness." Is it possible that our society might be suffering "consciousness"?

71

Back in the spring of 1992 a quote came out of Congress: "A balanced budget is only for the truly religious, for the balance to which it refers occurs only in the hereafter."

There are those who simply do not believe that God's Kingdom has a chance in this world, and, believe me, I have my days. But I do believe these words from Archbishop William Temple, written in 1930:

> *While we deliberate, God reigns; when we decide wisely, God reigns; when we decide foolishly, God reigns; when we serve God in humble loyalty, God reigns; when we serve God self-assertively, God reigns; when we rebel and seek to withhold our service, God reigns — the Alpha and the Omega, which is, and which was, and which is to come, the Almighty.*
>
> (From *Context*, February 1, 1992)

It's a marvelous mystery, isn't it, that on the one hand God works in spite of us, and on the other hand we are central to the plan God has of bringing salvation and wholeness to our world. Jesus didn't call his disciples to go with him by saying, "Come with me so we can stand around and watch God do mighty things." No, Jesus said, "Come with me and we'll go fishing, only now we'll fish for people instead of food for the tummy."

Jesus made it clear that there are some specific things for men and women to do, ministries which God uses to do kingdom-building work: like feeding the hungry, clothing the naked, aiding the poor, visiting those in prison, witnessing to everyone about God's love revealed in Jesus.

But for many in our society darkness prevails, as in Isaiah's day. Other gods than the Lord are being worshipped. Other ways of life than the way for which we are created are being followed.

Douglas Taylor-Weiss, rector of St. Andrew's Episcopal Church in Dayton, Ohio, has proposed a new set of Ten Commandments based on his observations of our culture. Here they are:

1. Have a good day.
2. Shop.
3. Eliminate pain.
4. Be up-to-date.
5. Relax.
6. Express yourself.
7. Have a happy family.
8. Be entertaining.
9. Be entertained.
10. Buy entertainment.
   (*Context,* February 1, 1992)

The fact is that those 10 commandments don't bring joy and meaning over a lifetime. God's commandments do. But what you and I know through God's gift of Jesus is that what God wants is not just people fearfully carrying out all God's commandments. What God wants is for us to know that God loves us with an everlasting love, as Jeremiah reminded his people in chapter 31, verse 3. We learn through Jesus that before we will be able to follow God's commandments, we must know, we must be converted to the reality of how much the Giver of those commandments loves us.

It is up to the church, and not to anyone else, to be sure that our country, our society, your business, your schoolmates, your children and family all get exposed to the great light, the message of Jesus Christ, the message that we are loved by God. Then we graciously give time and opportunity to allow our society to adjust to the light, for the darkness in which we live is so deep, that the pain of the light can be too great to bear. I believe an awareness of that one fact will help to give us patience and gentleness in our Christian witness.

Some of that adjusting to the light, I believe, is already happening. In some places, in some cities, in some communities, in some schools, the bright truth of God's love and way of life that brings meaning and joy is coming to be seen through squinted eyes.

The church must not lose its courage to witness even when it takes decades for people to catch on, to adjust to the light. I am glad that I am a part of a movement that is so monumental, so vast, so cosmic, so all encompassing, that it cannot be accomplished in my lifetime, a movement that is nothing less than the salvation of the world.

How Costly Grace?
Or
Does Spelling Count?

As long as men and women and boys and girls have inhabited this planet, they have sought to control their lives in whatever ways possible.

In order to have a better harvest, they have experimented with different crops, different fertilizers, and different methods of planting. In order to kill more game for food, they created more and more advanced kinds of bows, more accurate arrows, more deadly traps. In order to protect themselves from neighboring tribes they produced walls and moats and castles, and better weapons.

But there has always been a feeling of uncertainty. A particular method of planting, a new brand of hunting instrument or weapon, a certain kind of house did not necessarily bring success. There were some things beyond their control. The crops might still fail, their enemies sometimes would still prevail, the arrow often missed the animal, and their children and loved ones still died of accident and disease.

Therefore, from the beginning of time there has been a search for a power beyond what humans themselves could muster, a power which could bring success and confidence and victory.

75

Also from the beginning of time there has been an awareness of a spiritual reality. Human beings have always been moved by key moments in their lives, and those moments have been the same for the first men and women who roamed the earth as for you and me today: birth, death, a spectacular sight in nature, a moment of terror and fear, a moment of grace and relief and gratitude. In such moments the human spirit has connected with **the** Spirit, the Spirit of the One we now know is God.

It's not surprising then that men, women, boys and girls have sought to influence the unseen presence beyond them, to help them in time of need, to protect them when afraid.

How might one decide how to influence a god? Wouldn't you start with how you influence another person? Of course. And so people began giving their gods things that were precious to them, assuming that such offerings would make the gods happy. And what are our most precious things? Well, that would be the cream of the crop, the best food, or, the very best, the most precious of all: one's very offspring, one's children. Therefore, child sacrifice was begun.

The Old Testament records the dawning of the awareness among the people called Hebrews, that there was not a number of gods, all with various powers, but rather there was one God, more powerful than all the others. This God created the world out of love and a desire to be in relation with us. Only later did they understand that there was only one God, period.

It was only natural then that some of the understanding from other pagan cultures would slip into their worship of this great Yahweh, the Lord. And one of the major traditions was offering sacrifices. Early in our scriptures we read of it in the tragic story of Cain and Abel. Cain felt that God liked Abel's animal offering better than Cain's offering of the fruit of the ground. Out of jealousy over what offering God liked better, the first murder was committed. God must have wept as he saw his creatures kill over such misguided understandings of what God desired of them.

Which brings us to the focus of this morning. What in the world does God want of us, for heaven's sake?

People down through the centuries have struggled with that question. Moses was given the Ten Commandments on Mount Sinai, a list of those basic guidelines for life which God has forever set down. But that still left lots of questions.

Hundreds of laws were written in an effort to respond to people's questions of specifically what God wanted of them, and what would make God "smile" on them. And finally, in the fullness of time, God sent us Jesus to make it clear that what God wants is not that we obey a list of laws, no matter how correct. Rather what God wants is that we love God with our whole being and that we love our neighbors, near and far, and ourselves. Everything else is fine print. And Jesus lived out that kind of life before the people of his time.

God did give some guidance prior to Jesus, however, though it was hidden in the midst of the laws and fears and sacrificial traditions of the Jewish people. The prophet Micah was a prophet from 742-687 B.C., a time period which over-lapped much of the ministry of Isaiah, including the period of the reign of King Hezekiah. The words of the prophet Micah, which we are looking at this morning, are considered by many to be one of the four or five mountaintop gems in all of scripture.

Before we get to that, though, I want to just mention what to me is the low point in all of scripture in the search for an answer to the question, "What does the Lord require of you?" It's right up there with Abraham's almost-sacrifice of Isaac.

I'm talking about what happened with Jephthah, the son of Gilead, who was asked by the Israelites to lead the battle against the Ammonites, some thousand years or so before Jesus' birth. The story is a terrible one. In order to gain the support of God, Jephthah said the following to God, as quoted in Judges 11:30-31:

> *If you will give the Ammonites into my hand, then whoever comes out of the doors of my house to meet me,*

77

when I return victorious from the Ammonites, shall be
the Lord's, to be offered up by me as a burnt offering.

Jephthah and his army defeated the Ammonites and home
he went rejoicing over the defeat. And coming out to meet
him, dancing with timbrels, glad to see her daddy home safe
and sound, was Jephthah's only child, his lovely daughter.

Seeing her father's face fall and learning the reason, the
unnamed daughter said, "My father, if you have opened your
mouth to the Lord, do to me according to what has gone out
of your mouth." And he did, though the details are mercifully left out, other than the moving verses 39-40: "So there arose
an Israelite custom that for four days every year the daughters of Israel would go out to lament the daughter of Jephthah
the Gileadite."

As long as there are people who believe that the God of
the universe is willing to be party to vows and bargains like
that of Jephthah, there will be people who will not consider
faith and trust in such a God. And for good reason!

The prophet Micah saw the religious sickness among his
people and after putting forth the rhetorical questions, listing
all the kinds of sacrifices which people had been wont to give,
burnt offerings, calves, thousands of rams, rivers of olive oil,
one's firstborn, Micah makes this statement, one of the highest
statements of religious truth in all of literature:

He has told you, O mortal, what is good;
and what does the Lord require of you
but to do justice, and to love kindness,
and to walk humbly with your God?

Justice and kindness in relations with people, and humility before God. That is what God wants of us. And that is what
Jesus lived out before us. He lived and taught justice, with
the poor, the rich, the sinners, and the scribes and Pharisees.
He lived and taught kindness, with children and women and
the sick. He even lived and taught humility before God, whose
very Son he was. When in talking about the end of the world,

he said, "Only the Father knows such timetables" (Matthew 27:36; Mark 13:32).

Justice and kindness and humilty before God.

The reality in our day which those of us in the church need to acknowledge and confess is that we are seen by the world as unjust in our treatment of other Christians and not involved enough in matters of justice in the world. We are seen as often supremely unkind toward people, particularly those who do not share our details of faith and doctrine. And we are seen as supremely cocky and arrogant and know-it-all in our relationship with God, when in fact, we of all people should be the most humble, for we know of the greatness and the mystery of God Almighty. It is we who should know the words of scripture from Isaiah 55:8 and 9:

> *For my thoughts are not your thoughts, nor are your ways my ways, says the Lord. For as the heavens are higher than the earth, so are my ways higher then your ways and my thoughts than your thoughts.*

Humility before God is the beginning of faith, and opens our hearts and minds up to search for how we may need to change in our thinking and our acting regarding ourselves and our neighbor. It may appear admirable to be absolutely certain about every bit of doctrine and every portion of scripture, but in fact the attitude of the follower of God is humility, utter humility.

Through God's gift of Jesus we know all we need to know for salvation, but that is not close to proclaiming that we know all there is to know about faith and doctrine. We all still look through a glass darkly, as Saint Paul has said. Only when we are with the Lord will we see face to face and know fully.

I remember once someone asking me in utter seriousness, "How much can I get away with and still go to heaven?" It reminded me of the question youth and children often ask before an exam: "Does spelling count?"

Micah says it is not a matter of adding up points and tallying up percentages of Sundays when you went to church or how often and what kind of sacrifices you offered to God. What does God want?

He has told you, O Mortal, what is good; and what does the Lord require of you but to do justice, and to love kindness, and to walk humbly with your God?
(Micah 6:8)

Through Jesus Christ this message has been underlined and finalized. There is nothing you have to do to earn God's love. No sacrifice, no ritual, no trick questions to answer will get us into the arms of God or earn us good health or convince God to do something for a loved one.

Yes, the grace, the loving, forgiving grace of God is costly, because it demands our whole allegiance, our whole selves. But we are not to replace that kind of wholesome, healthy, lifegiving commitment to the way of God in Christ with a poor, sick substitute of something God would never ask of us, such as the lifeless body of a child or the paltry offering of a few good deeds or a string of perfect attendance pins, or even the ability to cling firmly to some proper doctrine set up by the church or denomination of our choice.

No, the life of faith comes from active, humble love, embracing both our neighbor and our God. And such a life of meaning and faith and joy may be found and experienced by walking in the footsteps of Jesus.

Epiphany 5
Isaiah 58:3-12

Cultivating Our Lenten Garden

I remember a news program which showed the release of a number of wild turkeys into the wilderness of southwestern United States. They were seeking to reestablish a strain of turkeys in that area. In order to track them and understand how they were doing, a little radio was affixed to the back of each of the turkeys. Can you imagine being able to sit at a screen and follow the whereabouts of all those turkeys?

How would you like to have a tracking device affixed to your back, so that your family, and your best friends, and your church community, and your bowling team and your lodge could follow your every move? Every day. How would you like that?

This thought occurred to me as I was thinking about this coming Lenten season, a time when, for centuries and centuries, Christians have either been preparing for their baptism on Easter, or they have been in a time of renewal, leading up to the great celebration of the resurrection of Jesus Christ. Where would a radio on my back track me this coming Lent, as I seek to deepen my walk with God?

Of course if we follow the advice of Micah the prophet, whose words we pondered last week, I would be out and about doing works of justice and kindness, not forgetting, as I do so, to walk humbly with God. That's what Micah said God wants.

This morning we hear the prophet Isaiah say some similar words about not carrying on with a selfish, ostentatious fast, but rather caring for the needs of others.

Some time ago in a denominational newspaper I read what a contemporary theologian, the Rev. Theodore Jennings, said. He spoke at a Minister's Week Lecture at Candler School of Theology in Atlanta. Surely he got everyone's attention with some statements he made about what he thinks we should be doing . . . or, should I say, **not** doing. Hold on to your pews.

"Being a Christian," said Dr. Jennings, "has nothing whatever to do with worship and what is now called liturgy . . ." In fact, he said, worship is often "positively dangerous to the health of faith discipleship . . . The idea that by going to church, by attending worship, we have thereby done something that places us in relation to the God of Jesus Christ is the most catastrophic delusion that infects the life of faith." Dr. Jennings wasn't done: "Jesus explicitly forbids his followers to pray in public. If you must be religious, he seems to say, then hide it away; never admit it in public" (*The United Methodist Review*, Vol. 11, No. 4, February 11, 1994).

There! Can you imagine the discussion Dr. Jennings started at that conference? I doubt if anyone fell asleep, either during his lecture or when they were trying to do so late at night!

While I believe Dr. Jennings has thrown the baby out with the bath water, I think he was trying to say what Jesus said in far fewer words: ". . . you will know them by their fruits. Not everyone who says to me, 'Lord, Lord,' will enter the kingdom of heaven, but only the one who does the will of my Father in heaven" (Matthew 7:21).

I have long had the suspicion, both for the church in general and sometimes for me in particular, that church activity and worship can become an insidious *ersatz,* or substitute, for real obedience to God's call to follow in the footsteps of Jesus.

This is the idea the author of the book of James is getting at in the second chapter.

> *What good is it, my brothers and sisters, if you say you have faith but do not have works? Can faith save you? If a brother or sister is naked and lacks daily food, and one of you says to them, "Go in peace; keep warm and eat your fill," and yet you do not supply their bodily needs, what is the good of that? So faith by itself, if it has no works, is dead.* (James 2:14-17)

What Dr. Jennings, in making his strong point, overlooks, however, is that the human person is more than just a mind that makes decisions. The human person also has a heart and emotions, and our difficulty in **doing** what's right, as Saint Paul has said in Romans 7, is precisely the difficulty, not just in knowing **what** to do. It is worship which, at its best, puts us in touch with God's Holy Spirit and with each other and with God's Word, so that we will be motivated to leave the sanctuary and **do** something for Christ's sake!

Even without overtly religious words and actions, watching the Winter Olympics' opening ceremony always makes me want to run out and do something to unite our broken world. Worship does not **just** motivate, but at its best, it does do so, and profoundly.

Isaiah was wrestling with the same issue as Dr. Jennings. In chapter 58, verse 2 he says: "... day after day [the house of Jacob] seek[s] me and delight[s] to know my ways, as if they were a nation that practiced righteousness and did not forsake the ordinance of their God..." Some pretty harsh words. He then goes on to criticize the way the people were fasting. Fasting, remember, was a religious act of devotion to God, including not eating for a period of time, but also, for some, putting on sack cloth and covering oneself with ashes. It was an act of worship and humbling oneself before God.

The trouble was that these same people, even while they were fasting, were serving their own interests, oppressing their workers and quarrelling and fighting. Isaiah then said that the fast which the Lord delights in is

> ... *to loose the bonds of injustice, to undo the thongs*
> *of the yoke, to let the oppressed go free ... to share your*
> *bread with the hungry and bring the homeless poor into*
> *your house; when you see the naked, to cover them ...*
> *then your light shall break forth like the dawn ...*
>
> (Isaiah 58:6, 7, 8)

Robert McAfee Brown wrote once that God "... works
through the prophets ... [and] even on occasion through the
church, which expends so much energy vainly trying to tame
a message whose radical dimensions keep showing through."
It is that radical dimension which makes us uncomfortable
sometimes, but it is also the radical dimension of the gospel
which, through God's Spirit, gives us new energy and new life.
Listen to the words of Isaiah:

> ... *if you offer your food to the hungry and satisfy the*
> *needs of the afflicted, then your light shall rise in the*
> *darkness and your gloom be like the noonday. The Lord*
> *will guide you continually, and satisfy your needs in*
> *parched places, and make your bones strong; and you*
> *shall be like a watered garden ...*
>
> (Isaiah 58:10-11)

The only way for worship to be worship is to be sure
that it comes bubbling up out of being in ministry in and to
our world in the name of Christ, bringing a cup of cold water
to those who hurt. And then, "Surprise!" that same cup of
water waters our own soul gardens.

Sounds pretty good compared with the barren gardens
we've sometimes created by avoiding mission and ministry by
"going to church." Something to ponder this Lent.

Training Wheels For Life

Another world, another day, another time. The bright sun cast its long dark shadows along streets filled with carts and animals, never once falling on automobile, trolley or McDonald's litter in the gutter.

Another world, another day, another time. Yet the sounds of people were there, even more evident without the sound of motor cars. The shouting of a young man, the call of an elderly woman, the bawling of a young child. But in the darkness of an entryway to a home on that busy street we see a door open, the top corner catching the sun's light as the door swings open into the fresh morning, smelling of wet dirt and dung.

An old but vibrant-looking man, dressed humbly, holds the door open as he asks questions of a diminutive lad pulling on trousers and pushing on cap with one hand as he clutches papers in the other.

"Come along now, or you'll be late!" urges the older gentleman, speaking those words so familiar to every day and time. And the youth behaves as have youth since the beginning of time on their way to school, busy about seemingly everything except for getting himself to school.

"Hi!" he shouts to a friend, waving. The older gentleman at his side swoops down and picks up the paper lost in the wave, and says the other words so ubiquitous over the eons. "I'm not going to tell you again, young man! Get a move on!" And down the street they go, the boy of ancient Palestine seemingly oblivious to everything *except* that which would make him late for school. Fortunately his family's hired servant was to see to it that he did, in fact, make it there punctually.

Who was this hired servant? The great Bible scholar, William Barclay, says that a Jewish household had a servant who was called the *paidagogos,* the one whose job it was to see to it that a family's children got their education and proper upbringing. It was not the *paidagogos'* job to give the children their education. Rather it was his job to see to it that the children got to the places of learning where their education could occur (Cf. *The Daily Bible Series,* Galatians and Ephesians, page 31).

A man who very likely grew up with his own *paidagogos,* Saint Paul, spent a good deal of precious parchment writing to the church at Galatia about one part of a Jew's upbringing, the thorough learning of the law. The term law held much more meaning than it does for you and me today. For the Jew it was that sacred bit of ancient scripture including the Ten Commandments and many other guidelines of faith and custom which the faithful Jew spent his or her life studying and trying obediently to follow. After many paragraphs of analogies and arguments, Paul says these words in Galatians 3:24: ". . . the law was our disciplinarian until Christ came . . ."

You have heard me say that to be a disciple of Jesus Christ is not just to follow a list of commandments, to simply *not* do some certain things. This morning I want to balance that with a word about the still important role of the commandments.

Toward the end of the book of Deuteronomy Moses finished his long discourse explaining all the rules and commandments and rituals which the Lord had told him to share with the Hebrews before they entered into the Promised Land, the land of milk and honey. One of the Lord's final words through Moses was this: "I call heaven and earth to witness against you today that I have set before you life and death, blessings and curses. Choose life so that you and your descendants may live" (Deuteronomy 30:19).

It is true, one does not have life simply by obeying commandments. That is what Peter told the gathering at the Council of Jerusalem as the new Christian church was sorting out what Jewish laws and customs new Christians had to obey. In Acts 15:10, in speaking specifically of the custom of circumcision, Peter said these words: "Now therefore why are you putting God to the test by placing on the neck of the disciples a yoke that neither our ancestors nor we have been able to bear?" At their worst, when customs and rituals are compulsively followed in order to appease God, they can be a burden and can, in fact, be a wedge between someone and God.

However, I would like to remind us this morning that God's commandments can also be our *paidagogos,* the disciplinarian keeping us in a place where we can grow in our relationship with God. Remember, it was the *paidagogos,* the servant, who saw to it that the child was in school where he could sit at the feet of the teacher.

I remember an interview during the Olympic winter games in Lillihammer. It was with one of the leaders of the U.S. Olympics. He was asked about how much credit for the success of the United States' team should rightfully go to the individual athletes and how much should go to the development and training program, the structure which got them the training they needed. An interesting question. The answer, of course, was both. But without the plan and the structure, the individuals never would have been as prepared as they were in Lillihammer. The training structure provided a place within which the individuals could develop their talent.

Commandments. "You shall have no other gods before me. You shall make no idol. You shall not take the name of the Lord your God in vain. Remember the Sabbath day to keep it holy. Honor your father and your mother. You shall not kill, commit adultery, steal, bear false witness or covet anything that is your neighbor's.''

Ten commandments. These are those parameters God has given us to enable us to be in a position to grow in our relationship with God and with our neighbor.

I like our lay leader's term, ''training wheels.'' Are the commandments not our training wheels, enabling us to move forward in our walk with God and neighbor? The commandments are training wheels for life, the real life of faith in Christ. The commandments discipline us so we are prepared to take the next steps, steps of faith, a walk lived not from shoulds and oughts, but rather from gratitude, love and joy, the walk of a disciple of Jesus Christ, the walk of a forgiven prodigal returning home, experiencing at last the love that had been there all along.

This Lent may I suggest that we give ourselves a daily Ten C check? Let us be our own *paidagogos,* disciplining ourselves so that learning of God can take place. Let us review daily how we're doing in following the ten commandments. You can find them in Exodus, chapter 20. It could be that there are those times in our lives when we ache to know the Lord, but by breaking so many of the basic commandments of life we are in fact living in a barren land far from God, instead of sitting in God's presence.

Let us use those most basic of God's guidelines as training wheels, and let us use them for life.

Living Our Lives On The Edge

In the course of my growing up I was in a great variety of clubs and groups. But no club had as stringent and compelling rules, and no club demanded daily attention to its guidelines for behavior and action quite as much as a particular club which met in our home. It met usually three times a day, and the meetings were always at meal time. I'm talking about The Clean Plate Club!

Now just in case there is someone here who missed out on membership in this exclusive club and therefore is uninformed as to its nature, let me explain. The club is really quite easy to describe and the rules are supremely easy to understand. The Clean Plate Club is composed of those proper boys and girls who eat everything that is dished up on their plate. It was always assumed, whether true or not, that every boy and girl would want to be a member of this exclusive organization, for my parents and grandparents would always say, "Finish what's on your plate. You want to be a member of the Clean Plate Club, don't you?" I didn't always, but I never said so. As I recall, my desire for membership in the Clean Plate Club seemed to depend on what exactly it was that needed to be cleaned up!

There were times, of course, when I was driven to membership in this club, and would climb under the table to ensure membership by licking the plate or bowl clean. I assumed that by doing so my mother would be particularly happy, in that she wouldn't have to wash that particular dish. But I digress.

My point in reminiscing with you this morning is that I believe there is evidence to suggest that there may well be a large percentage of the population of the world who enjoy membership in this same club of which I speak.

You see, the point of this club is to search out and find the last morsel of food which lies on the eater's plate, and consume it. And it would appear to me that many of us have that same compulsion in other areas of our lives. Let me explain.

It has been my experience that when I'm at a Thanksgiving meal and watch the server of the pies dish out my delicious piece of apple or pumpkin pie (usually a piece of both), if they miss a tiny part of what should be my piece, I frown inside and long with an eager longing for that little tiny morsel I missed. Or I may gather up my loins and say gently and/or firmly, depending on who the server is, "Er, ah, may I have it **all**, please?" Can any of you pie lovers relate to that?

I have also discovered that if I receive an unexpected windfall of money, say $25, and there's a special offering coming up in church for some worthy cause, I still find that it takes a lot of effort to say, "Heck, I wasn't expecting this money anyway, I'll just give it all to this worthy cause."

Do you see what I mean? It's that strong training in the Clean Plate Club that's doing it. What's mine should be **all** mine, especially those last few morsels. Why, to be honest, those last few morsels feel more rightfully mine than all the rest!

Apparently the Clean Plate Club has been around influencing people for a long time, because the same problem demanded some attention centuries before Jesus was born. Indeed, way back in the days of Moses at the edge of recorded history, the Lord was trying to deal with the results of that ancient club.

I'm thinking of how the Lord chose to deal with it through the servant Moses, as recorded in the third book of the Bible, Leviticus. The book is called Leviticus because it has much to do with work and the ministry of the Levitical priests.

Chapter 19 of Leviticus begins with the Lord's call to all the people of Israel to be holy. Why? Because God is holy and they were God's children. This portion of Leviticus, as you noted I'm sure, repeats some of the parts of the Ten Commandments. But the part I want to lift up for our attention this morning is verse 9, which has to do with the issue I've been talking about:

> *When you reap the harvest of your land, you shall not reap to the very edges of your field, or gather the gleanings of your harvest. You shall not strip your vineyard bare, or gather the fallen grapes of your vineyard; you shall leave them for the poor and the alien: I am the Lord your God.*

The word of the Lord which Moses shared with his people was that one should not be a member of the Clean Plate Club when it came to gathering all the produce and wealth that belonged to his people. Rather, one should nurture an attitude of generosity, leaving the corners uncut, leaving bunches of grain here and there for those who had nothing, so they could come along and glean for themselves later. To leave some for others was to be holy, and generous, like their God.

The whole business of gleaning came alive for me when I was living in the country in western New York some years ago. Right across from the church there was a large field which was planted annually by a company that raised green beans. When the time for harvest came we would see these huge dinosaur-like pieces of machinery arrive to pick the beans and spit them out into a huge cage, which would then be dumped into enormous trailers.

What I learned in all that was that there were many folks who waited for that harvest day and would move in after the "dinosaurs" were gone to pick the beans that were left. Modern day gleaning.

Of course the most colorful and interesting story about gleaning comes from the Old Testament book of Ruth, in which Ruth gleaned all day in the fields for her mother-in-law Naomi, eventually marrying Boaz, the owner of the fields.

But back to Leviticus. The Lord called the people of Israel to a life of generosity, remembering when they were wandering in the wilderness themselves after they escaped from Egypt, and had nothing to eat. The Lord called them to think beyond themselves, and to be grateful for the abundance of food and goods that was theirs, that those less fortunate might be cared for. It was sort of the welfare system of their day.

Remember Jesus' parable of the rich man whose harvest one year was so enormous that he decided to tear down the barns he had and build bigger ones to hold it all? Luke records the story in the 12th chapter. Remember the man then said, ". . . I will say to my soul, 'Soul, you have ample goods laid up for many years; relax, eat, drink, be merry.' " Jesus suggests that an attitude of simply stockpiling all you can in order to "eat, drink and be merry" is not an attitude that brings one close to God and one's neighbor, and it leads to a hollow life.

It really struck me as I was studying this portion of Leviticus, that we really do tend to spend much of our time and energy on the edges of our resources, scratching and clawing for every last penny or dollar, no matter how big the harvest has been in our lives. Whether our resources are great or whether they are meager, it would seem that there is a Clean Plate Club attitude, that drives us to walk the fields of our resources, being sure we didn't miss anything, being sure that nothing is left that someone else might get.

I needn't tell you, of course, that the amount of resources a person has is never related to how generous a person is. No, it is the ones with the most generous hearts, filled with gratitude to God for all their blessings, large and small, who love to give with abandon.

I'll never forget a story I read once about rescue workers in a famine-stricken area who were handing out glasses of milk to some half-starved orphans. One was a little boy who had several brothers and sisters and was used to having to divide his food with them. He asked the worker who gave him the milk, "How far down can I drink?"

"All the way down, Honey," she said. "All the way down!"

The problem is that there are those of us who are drinking from huge glasses, compared to 95 percent of the rest of the world, and we, too, insist on drinking "all the way down."

I believe we could find great joy by being a more centered people, not frantically combing the edges of potential resources for something we have missed, but rather grateful to God for all that we do have. Such a life inevitably leads to an overflowing love for our neighbor and leads to walking in the footsteps of Jesus.

Traveling Forgotten Mountains

Larry Crabb has written a book called *Moving Through Your Problems Toward Finding God.* In the foreword the author writes,

> *I have come to a place in my life where I need to know God better or I won't make it. Life at times has a way of throwing me into such blinding confusion and severe pain that I lose all hope. Joy is gone. Nothing encourages me ... The rhetoric we're all used to — "just trust the Lord, pray more, get counseling, follow God's plan more carefully" — must give way to the reality of finding God.*

Dr. Crabb goes on to say that we don't feel we can trust God. "We thank him for opening up a parking place in a crowded lot, but we cannot trust him with our souls" (page 95). Perhaps you can relate to these words of Dr. Crabb.

Seven and a half centuries before Christ, or about 2,700 years ago, there was another writer who was trying to speak to a people thrown into "blinding confusion and severe pain," a whole people for whom all hope was lost, joy was gone, a people for whom nothing seemed to provide encouragement.

These people were the Israelites who had been exiled from their homeland, Palestine, by the Babylonians. Can you imagine being tossed out of your hometown and forced to live in a state hundreds of miles away? The favorite drifts for bass just a memory. Your home which was so carefully built and landscaped destroyed by an invading enemy ...

It was in the midst of this hopelessness, in the midst of exile in Babylon that Isaiah wrote this hope-filled chapter. "Thus says the Lord: In a time of favor I have answered you, on a day of salvation I have helped you ..." (Isaiah 49:8).

This was quite a word of promise at a time when those in exile were saying, "The Lord has forsaken us, our Lord has forgotten us."

Is that not the feeling of many today? I talked with someone recently who said she knew few people who were really happy. Problems seem to be everywhere.

In his wonderful little book, *Your God Is Too Small*, J.B. Phillips writes,

> *To some people the mental image of God is a kind of blur of disappointments. "Here ... is One whom I trusted, but He let me down." The rest of their lives is consequently shadowed by this letdown. Thenceforth there can be no mention of God, Church, religion, or even parson, without starting the whole process of association with its melancholy conclusion: God is Disappointment.*
> (p. 48)

On our final evening together at a confirmation class retreat, we spent a good deal of time dealing with the feelings of disappointment over God's "poor handling" of the world. Surely there were Israelites in exile in Babylon who had given up on this God who didn't seem to care for them, who seemed to have forgotten them.

My dear friends, the feeling of being forgotten by God has been a feeling which everyone through the centuries has known, when things were at their worst. The saints called it "the dark night of the soul.'' Even our Lord cried out from the cross, "My God, my God, why have you forsaken me?'' This was not the last word, but it was a very real feeling in that moment, for sure.

The question is how do we travel those arduous, painful, exhausting mountain trails of loneliness and despair, of feeling forgotten by God, when no AAA Triptik reveals a detour, a better road?

Isaiah writes with great flair and confidence in verse 11 of chapter 49 that the Lord would turn all mountains into roads. That is, the very things that appear to be obstacles would end up being helpful roads to aid us in our journey.

I suspect the greatest lie that has been both preached and believed is that to become a Christian, to be a disciple of Jesus, is to have a piece of plastic in one's hip pocket that can be shown in hospital, doctor's office, bedroom, living room, place of work and place of stress that staves off death, pain and uncertainty. Just show the card! "Here, see! I'm a Christian. I get to go through without pain.''

Nowhere in the Bible or in the teachings of Jesus is such drivel taught. Rather we learn through Jesus that the key to successful and joyful living is a close relationship with the God of the universe and our neighbors. And that only comes through a conscious decision to spend our lives seeking to know God, with Jesus as our guide.

Loneliness is a real feeling that Jesus felt and we feel. But it is a feeling, not a description of God's location or lack of existence.

If you want a crazy, fun, deep, moving, spiritually enriching novel to read, find *The River Why*, by David James Duncan. Your pleasure in reading it may be heightened if you like to fish, but anyone whose heart is beating will be enriched by it.

At one point toward the end of the book the main character, Gus, is in a conversation with Nick, an older man who had been making fishing rods and tying flies with him for some months in his little cabin in a remote part of Oregon. Just before Nick moves away, Gus gets up the nerve to ask Nick about the scar on one of his palms. In front of a warm fire Nick tells his story.

He served on a mine sweeper in the North Sea during WWII. He told Gus about how much he hated the chaplain who was always spouting off pious words of faith to him. Nick couldn't be less interested in such stuff. He then told of encountering a huge storm which tossed the relatively little ship like a cork on a pond. After a sleepless night of being tossed about, Nick got up for duty just as dawn was breaking. They had steered a course into the lee of the Norwegian mountains to wait out the storm. Suddenly, about a mile off the coast they hit a floating mine, blowing the front of the hull away and sinking the ship with most of its crew in minutes.

Nick ended up in the water, more or less in shock and soon numb from the cold water. To make the long and gripping story short, a big trawler eventually appeared and after taking on a number of the survivors, Nick saw a man with a short stubby fishing pole cast his line out past him. He could see the line but he couldn't feel it, nor could he grasp it, for there was no feeling in his hands.

As the line was being reeled in, the bobber moved by him and he tried to enfold his body around it, but could not hold on. Then he saw it, a five-inch, heavy gauge hook. The ship was pulling away and it was his last chance. As best as he could he held the point of the hook against his palm, waiting for the line to come taut ... it did, and mercifully he soon blacked out as he was literally reeled into the boat.

Gus found out where the scar on Nick's hand came from, a scar that was the remaining evidence of how he was hauled to safety. And for Nick, that experience changed his life. Listen to his final words to Gus:

> *It isn't that it would have been so bad for me to drown ... what scares me, what makes me happy, is what I'd have died believin' then, compared to what I'll die believin' now ... I don't know how to put it. I'm still not religious, never will be. But since this hook pierced me*

the world hasn't been the same. I just didn't know any-
thing, nothing at all, till God let me watch that line run
away from me, my hands all powerless an' cold. You're
young, Gus. I don't know if you've been to that place
beyond help or hope. But I was there, on the sea that
day. And I was sent the help unlooked for, an' it came
in the shape of a hook. An' nothin' will ever be the way
it was before that day, not for me it won't ...

It seems that, for reasons none of us can understand, the mountains of despair and loneliness, of being forgotten, often become the road to our connection with God. But often we have to make some tough decisions in the midst of our despair, trusting that God will honor the risks and the pain. Only you know what those risks are for you. For Nick it was facing pain in his hand, and it left a scar.

For Jesus it was facing death on a cross, and that, too, left wounds in his palms and feet and side. Yet out of such trust in God's faithfulness came our salvation.

Remember Isaiah's words in chapter 49, the fifteenth and sixteenth verses? He said, "Can a woman forget her nursing child, or show no compassion for the child of her womb? Even these may forget, yet I will not forget you. See, I have inscribed you on the palms of my hands ..."

One of the ways students in school remind themselves of the assignment for the coming week is to write it on their hands! Impossible to forget. Perhaps this is the image to take with you: a loving God taking pen in hand and writing on the almighty palm your every need.

With that confidence we all can travel our mountains of despair, of feeling forgotten, putting our hand in the hand of the one who will never leave us or forsake us, for we are inscribed on the palm of God.

Transfiguration Of The Lord
Exodus 24:12-18

From A Distance

Heroes are a part of the human experience. They motivate, stimulate, encourage, and provide role models. There's something about looking up to the one who did something that is so far beyond most everyone's reach or ability. "Wow! I could never do that!" we say.

All through the Olympics my wife and I joked about what we would look like if we tried to jump off the ski jump or leap into the air with skates on! It's remarkable what some people are able to do, and do it with grace and apparent ease. Can you do a back flip on a narrow beam of wood and leather? I still say it's impossible, even though I've seen it with my own eyes.

Some of that hero stuff was going on in the story we heard read this morning. Here's Moses, who's already a hero from leading the Hebrews out of Egypt. Now we see him, with Joshua, climbing up a mountain to be with God. The mountain becomes covered with a cloud, the glory of God, for six days, and then, on the seventh day Moses is called to go into the cloud to receive the commandments.

What struck me this last time I read this portion of scripture was the seventeenth verse: "Now the appearance of the glory of the Lord was like a devouring fire on the top of the mountain in the sight of the people of Israel.''

To the people of Israel, gathered at the foot of Mount Sinai, not only did they see a cloud, they saw a fire; and not only was it a fire, it was a "devouring fire." From where they stood at the bottom of the mountain, God looked like a frightening, flaming, consuming inferno.

Now put this together with the words of Saint Paul in the New Testament, whose mind and heart had been grasped by the spirit of Jesus. In speaking to the people of Athens about God, Paul said this: "... indeed [God] is not far from each one of us. For 'In him we live and move and have our being'; as even some of your own poets have said, 'For we too are his offspring.' "

For centuries people have sought to carry out commandments of God brought to them by their heroic holy people, and in doing so have felt very close to their guilt and fear and frustration over not being able to carry out the rules, but have felt very far from the One whose anger they were trying to avoid by carrying out those rules.

And then there is the other reaction to this distant God. Out of ignorance and fear there are those who simply conjure up what they hope God might be, which is usually a warm, cuddly grandpa, whose only desire is to make you happy.

A fearful, unapproachable, fire-breathing God, or a harmless, comfortable, wimp. Such are the usual images of God, when experienced ... at a distance.

I think it was during Desert Storm that the song "From A Distance" came out, sung by Bette Midler. It was a beautiful song, sung on the radio, sung in religious gatherings. It grabbed our longing for peace and indeed how peaceful and in harmony the earth looks ... from a distance.

Unfortunately the concluding part of the song, while sounding beautiful, carried a content of enormous heresy and, even worse, I wonder how many people even felt the jolt. Remember how it ended? "God is watching us, God is watching us, God is watching us ... **from a distance.**"

102

Now for Edward Herbert, the father of Deism, and Voltaire, both of the seventeenth and eighteenth centuries, and Thomas Paine, an American, also in the late eighteenth century, this song could have been their theme song. You see, Deism is one of the religious views of the Enlightenment which taught that God or the Deity created the world and then left it to itself, not intervening in any way in the affairs of nature or humanity. Yes, there's a God, says Deism, but to say that is only a philosophical statement about where the world comes from, not a statement of faith or trust in a present Spirit who cares and empowers and loves all created beings today. Deism teaches that, at best, God is watching us, *at a distance.*

This is not the present, loving God whom we come to know in the life, death and resurrection of Jesus. It describes our feelings of God's absence at times, for sure, but how we feel at our worst moments is not the foundation on which we build our whole understanding of God.

In fact, you see, the ''success'' of Moses and Joshua on Mount Sinai, and Peter, James and John with Jesus on the Mount of Transfiguration may not just be the fact that they were special (which they were!). What may in fact be a major part of their ''success'' at having a mountaintop experience is how they got to where they had that experience.

Think about it. They climbed and climbed and climbed and climbed. They had a goal of climbing that mountain and meeting the Lord. Meanwhile, the people were down on the plain, doing their thing and admiring their leaders who were putting some sweat and trust into their walk with God.

I don't pretend to say that if I put in the same effort as Scott Hamilton, I, too, could do a triple jump. But I'll bet I would amaze my family and friends and myself with how much I could do on skates if I put the same effort and time in it as Scott did. The question is motivation.

God is watching us, but if it is at a distance, frankly, I could care less. For I need One upon whom I can lean and turn to for real live help and guidance and strength. A God at a distance doesn't do it, and that's what Jesus came to explain to those trying to please a distant, angry-appearing God with their careful following of kosher laws and Sabbath regulations. Such rule-following does little when your life is on the line. When your life is on the line, you need solid reason to hope.

On December 17, 1927, off Provincetown, Massachusetts, the US destroyer *Paulding* rammed the US submarine *S-4*. In one of the most harrowing rescue attempts known to this part of the world, divers went up and down in gale force winds trying everything possible to rescue the six remaining men trapped in the forward torpedo room. The other 30 men had already died in other parts of the ship. In the blackness of that small space, with carbon dioxide levels ever rising, Morse code messages were sent from divers to trapped men and back again, tapped out with wrenches and hammers. One of the last messages from the forward torpedo room was tapped out by Lieutenant Graham Fitch, "Is there any hope?" The answer they received back was, "There is hope." And everything possible was done to save them, though time and rough seas finally doomed them. Not Navy rules of order but hope is what they lived on, in those final hours of blackness.

Remember when Dorothy and her friends went to find the Wizard of Oz to get her back to Kansas and provide her friends with appropriate body parts? Remember how, filled with hope, she approached the Wizard, and then little Toto pulled back a curtain, revealing a pudgy old man, moving levers and talking into a microphone. She discovered that the great Wizard was only a little man with a fancy machine. Remember how devastated she was? "You mean there isn't any Wizard? You mean there is no hope to get back to Kansas?"

In fact, when the little Totos of experience and friendships and study pull back the curtain, exposing our imagined wimpy God or our wrathful, fiery God, we find a God like Jesus. But we find not a powerless pretender, but rather a gentle Lord, worthy of our praise and worship, and wielding power and justice in ways far beyond our most ardent efforts to understand.

There is hope and there *is* a One like Jesus revealed. And that One lives not far away but closer than our very breath, in life and in life beyond this life. It's just that we may need to do some mountain climbing together to close the distance.